FABRIC

DEDICATIONS
To my good friend Georgina Cardew – EH
To Drew Barton Cliff – SC

First published in Great Britain in 2002 by
Pavilion Books
64 Brewery Road
London
N7 9NT

A member of **Chrysalis** Books plc

Designed by Stafford Cliff
Picture Research by Nadine Bazar
Special Photography by Dominic Blackmore
Product Sourcing and Research by Sarita Sharma

Quotation credits: pp8–9 *Texture Material* by
Vladimir Markov (translated by Maria Laakso),
(Union of Youth, 1914); pp64–65 *Sensual Home*
by Ilse Crawford, (Quadrille, 1997); pp126–127
*Complete Book of Paint and Decorative
Techniques* by Kevin McCloud (Ebury Press, 1996).

A CIP catalogue record for this book is
available from the British Library.

ISBN 1 86205 373 1

Printed and bound at Imago PTE Ltd, Singapore

2 4 6 8 10 9 7 5 3 1

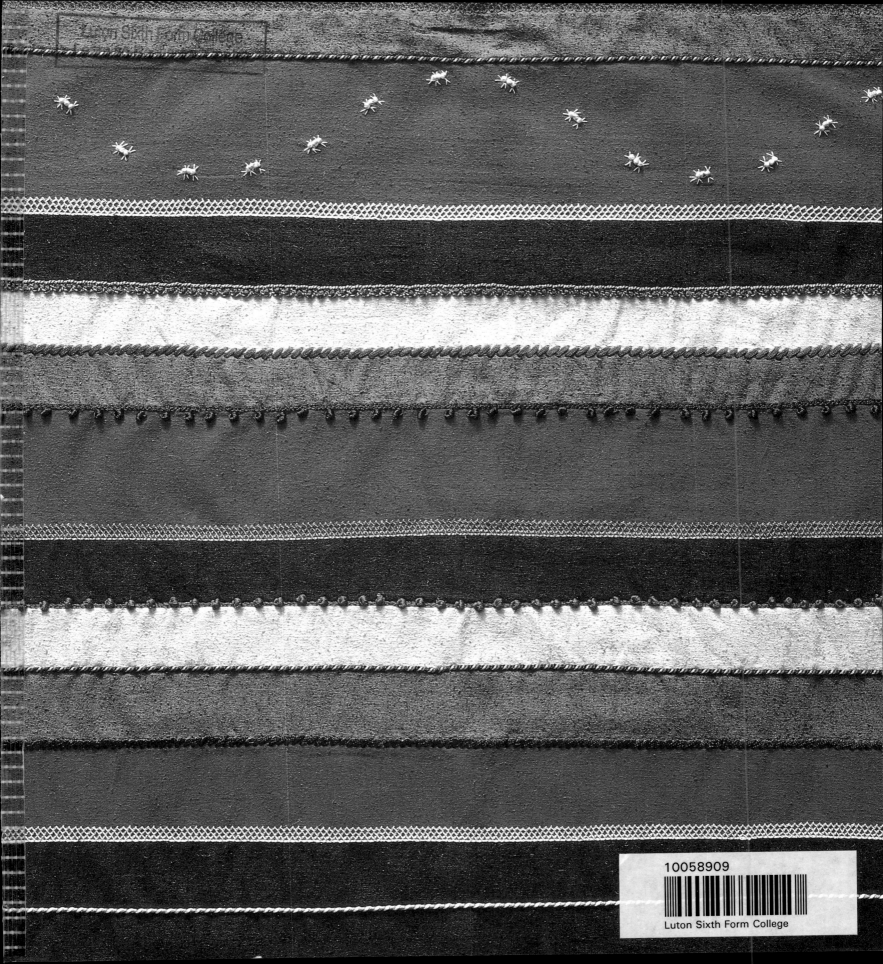

ELIZABETH HILLIARD AND STAFFORD CLIFF

FABRIC

THE FIRED EARTH BOOK OF NATURAL TEXTURE

PAVILION

'From the beginn
nature has been
materials and c
Organic life on e
of constantly ch

ing of time,
processing all
reating textures.
arth is a chaos
anging textures.'

Vladimir Markov

forget

fabric

think

texture

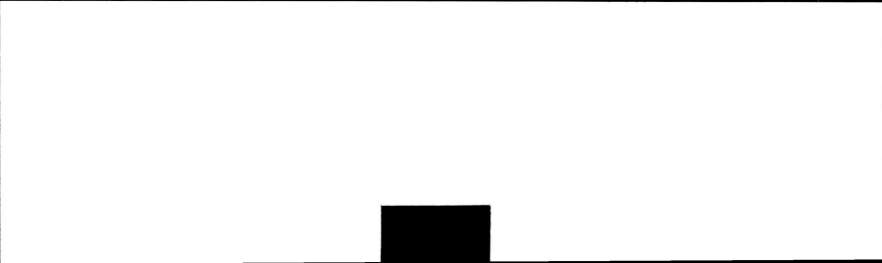

now think of some more

14

moss glass gravel sandpaper
lichen wicker ware woolly jumper
hedge tinsel bayleaf biscuit
breadcrumbs concrete cardboard
brick feather slate leather skin
cornflakes stainless steel rope
rose petal pine needles orange
peel terracotta snowflake sisal
silk stocking parchment loofah
pineapple mother-of-pearl bath
towel bowler hat cricket bat
sable string bird's nest birch
bark real sponge bubblewrap
tabby cat hammock ice cream
cone hairbrush tissue paper
porcupine bristle thistle potato
crisp cactus crew cut lettuce
leaf mushroom mown grass

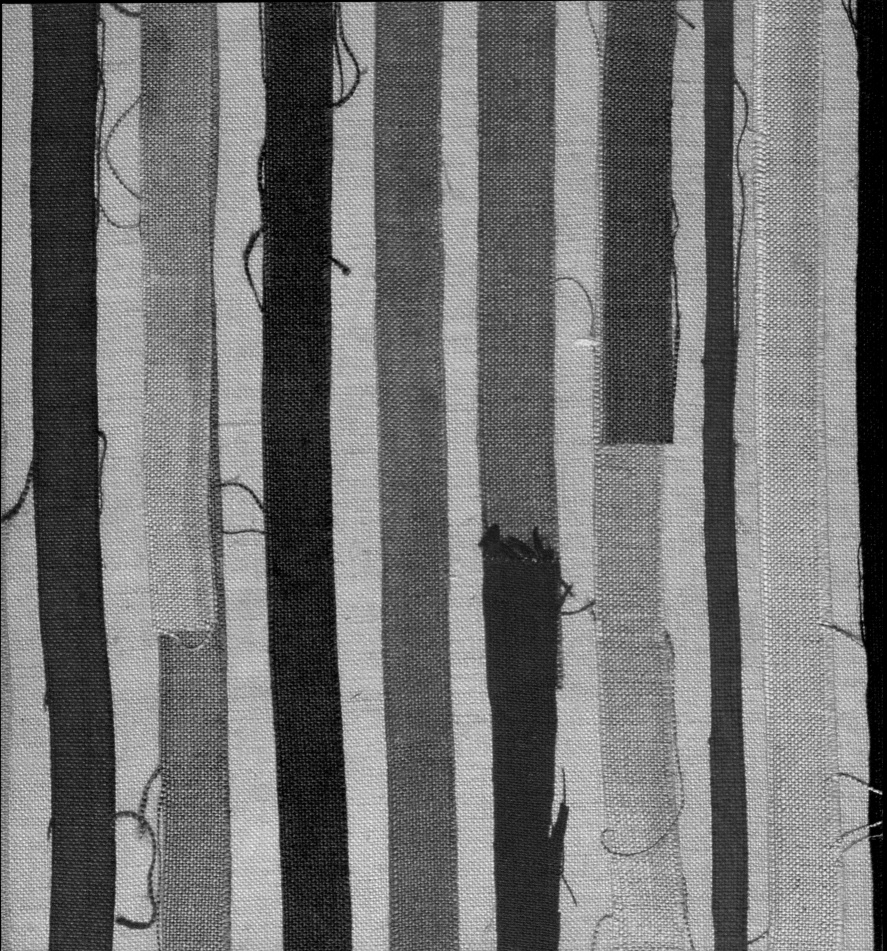

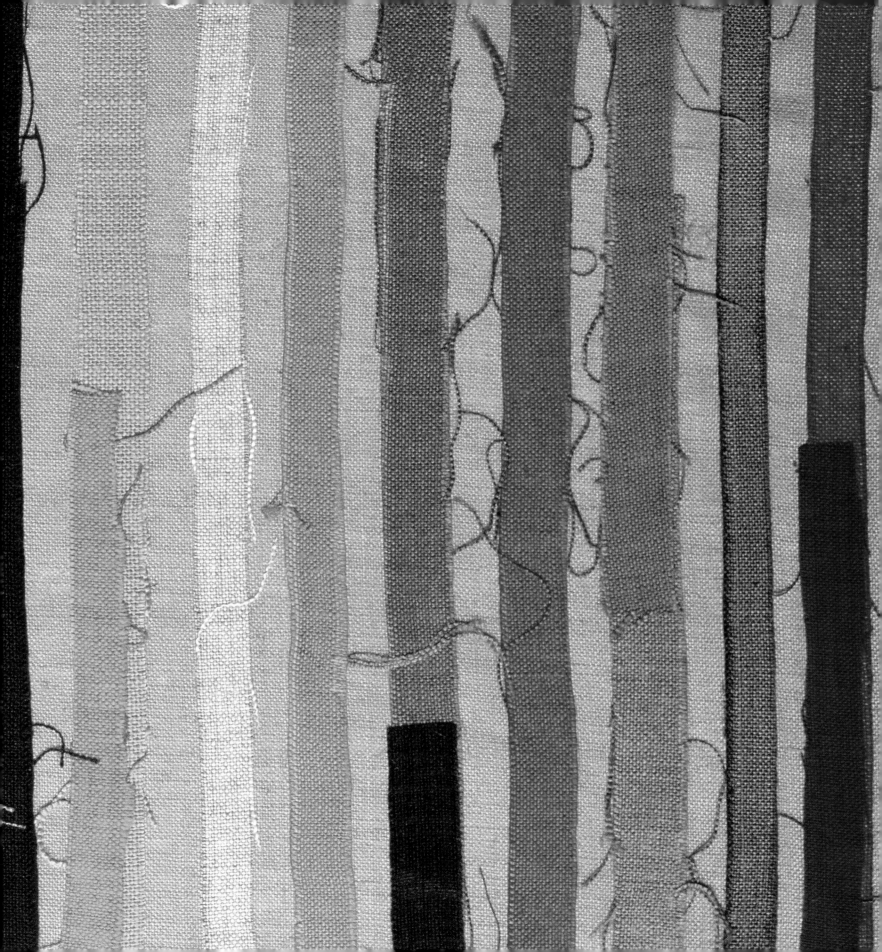

Introduction Of all the wonderful materials we use to construct and decorate our homes, the one that brings comfort and ease, softness and warmth, flexibility and fluidity, is fabric. How cold and hard our rooms would be without it! We may rejoice in the beauty of plain polished wood or stone and plaster, but we would live in chilly spaces indeed were we without the pleasurable indulgence of fabric. Every surface has a texture, but it is fabric that brings texture into our homes in a form we actually touch and feel. Fabric's wonderful variety of textures, from rough, slubby linen to warm, soft velvet and shimmering, sleek sheers... these bring our rooms, and us, alive through their feel, their play with light and the atmosphere they create.

Contemporary decorating is all about creating mood and effect. The textures of surfaces, together with their colour, are key to this, and none is more influential or desirable than the texture of fabric. Texture is a quality of which we have surprisingly little experience. In our daily lives, we mostly touch hard things made from plastic, metal, china and glass. Variety is provided by our clothes, and our food and drink. Compare this with the abundance of visual stimulus we enjoy every day. Our sense of sight is flooded with colour and images from the world around us, from the media, cinema, travel, art. In none of these do we experience much by touch – it is rare, for example, to be invited to feel the surface of a work of art. To curl up on a sofa, wrapped in a throw made from fleece or alpaca, or to snuggle against chenille-covered cushions, is really to feel texture. Bedlinen matters because it provides the fabric texture with which we are most fully in touch. To feel in this way is glorious.

But there is much more to fabric than just the sensation of touch. Texture cannot be divorced from the way the surface looks. Contrast a matt-pile fabric such as velvet whose surface captures light in its depths with a gleaming silk or satin, or a metallic sheer which reflects the light, bouncing it away. Some fabrics like muslin and perforated patterns allow the light through, teasing us playfully by veiling rather than concealing.

As well as the way a fabric feels and looks, its texture has associations for us which further deepen its significance in an interior. We only need to see a sofa covered with an angora throw to anticipate the embrace of softness, warmth and luxury. We only need to see linen sheets on a bed to yearn for their cool, relaxing touch on our skin at the end of a wearing day. The sight of these textures brings remembered pleasure and hence the desire for them to be repeated.

Some fabrics have wider associations. Chunky, hairy tweeds remind us of fresh air, weekend country walks, freedom from responsibility in the great outdoors. Elegantly watered silk immediately puts us in mind of a sophisticated drawing room, champagne, music, conversation, laughter late at night. These are mostly traditional and historical associations. Though they charm us, they need not constrain us in the way we use these or any fabrics, beyond the practical considerations relating to their performance. Leather, for example, was once used as (and still carries nostalgic echoes of) upholstery on deep, squashy old armchairs in the male preserves of libraries and smoking rooms in great country houses. Then it became a vital ingredient in the Modernist interior of the 1920s, used in black with chrome-finished tubular steel in the style of Charlotte Perriand, Le Corbusier and Eileen Gray. Today, leather is as likely to be brightly coloured or with a witty metallic finish, panelling the walls as well as upholstering the furniture in a fashionable city nightclub. Traditional black and brown leather and piebald ponyskin have been rediscovered and once again have a place in our homes, covering not just sofas and daybeds but floor cushions, beanbags and ottomans that double as occasional tables.

The sensuous enchantment which fabric textures so powerfully induce is thus not only connected with touch – it is also visual, remembered, anticipatory, associative. To feel (in the sense of to touch) and feeling (in the sense of our inner emotions) are closely interwoven, not by coincidence. Because they have this added resonance, textures offer us an invaluable tool in creating a particular atmosphere or mood in a room's decoration. Fabrics like satin and leather bring glamour to a room – others like fleece, jersey and faux fur embrace and pamper, creating a sumptuous mood of luxury and comfort. Fabric that is translucent or even perforated creates a dreamy impression, while fringed rubber and origami paper amaze and delight. Texture gives today's interior its character, depending on whether the fabrics are subtle or shiny, silky or spangled. Contrasts between textures heighten our delight in their individuality.

The traditional approach to using fabric to decorate your home focuses almost exclusively on two elements, pattern and colour. These are still extremely important in contemporary decorating, but they are no longer seen as qualities separate from texture. In the depths of an indigo-dyed hemp or the radiance of an iridescent sheer nylon, a slubby woven raffia or a finely embroidered cotton, the pattern and colour of the material cannot be separated from the surface qualities that compose its texture. Whether in large quantities, covering whole walls of windows, or in subtle details such as a single exquisite cushion, the texture of fabric brings light and depth, life and variety into our homes and our lives. Texture, alongside form and function, is a vital concern of the innovative textile designers and engineers in the USA, Japan and elsewhere who strive to push forward frontiers in the creation of new fabrics. Today, all forms of texture such as leather, paper and rubber are included in the overall term 'fabric'.

In ages past, textiles were used to express status and for decoration, certainly, but also served an important practical purpose – the preservation of heat. Curtains made of warm, heavy fabrics and fibres such as wool will never lose their usefulness as draught excluders in older buildings. But in the ultimate contemporary home, complete with double or triple glazing and underfloor heating, warmth is no longer the prime consideration. Fabric can be appreciated for itself, seen for its own inherent beauty. It is hung flat, or lightly gathered; upholstery is smooth rather than ruffled or buttoned so that the fabric is clearly seen and enjoyed. Rather than practical warmth, fabric brings to an interior fluidity and fun, providing potential for drama and seduction. It brings coolness and calm with neutrals and pale tones, or excitement with vibrant or ethnic colour and pattern.

Flamboyantly overblown window treatments and buttoned upholstery in the spirit of Empire and Victorian interiors are still an option – if that's what you really want. But this is the age of choice. Gone is any sense of social propriety or prestige in our choice of fabric. Today, we are free to upholster a chair in blue denim or to leave the linen of our loose covers intentionally unironed, positively relishing their crush and crumple. We are free to enjoy the look and feel of the latest astonishing techno-textiles, be they washable faux suede in exotic colours or bedsheets whose microfibre content will help ensure a peaceful night's sleep.

The origins of our love of using textured fabric to decorate our homes, and our appreciation of fabric's intrinsic beauty are twofold, drawn from opposite sides of the globe – the western concept of comfort on the one hand, the Japanese aesthetic on the other. The influence of Japanese design and ideas on western interior decoration in the late twentieth century and early twenty-first has been hugely important. This has promoted a pared-down, 'less is more' attitude to the decoration and furnishing of our homes, including the use of fabric. Have fewer possessions; strive for simplicity; count quality more important than quantity; honour the thought and labour that have gone into making something, at the same time as relishing the materials from which it has been formed. There is a resonance here of William Morris's exhortation to 'Have nothing in your home that you do not know to be useful or believe to be beautiful' (*The Beauty of Life*, 1880). Most obviously, of course, it strikes a chord with minimalism.

In Japanese culture, the best craftwork is revered as equal to art – textile technology is touched with this same sense of reverence and enthusiasm. We see this in the attitude to fabric of Japan's leading fashion designers whose names (rather than the names of Japanese interior decorators) are familiar to us. Nothing illustrates this better than the astonishing creations of Issey Miyake, supported by his textile designer Makiko Minagawa. Miyake does not simply use existing textiles to create sculptural garments – he invents new fabrics and finishes, such as his famously good-looking, comfortable, easy-care, heat-pleated polyester. Inventively pleated and tucked fabrics reminiscent of Fortuny silks (as are Miyake's pleats) are now to be found in interiors, usually covering cushions. (The cushion is an ideal micro-unit on which to display a piece of intricately decorated fabric.) Another Japanese genius of outstanding influence is Rei Kawakubo of Comme des Garçons. Her textile work was preceded by study of aesthetics and philosophy, underlining the Japanese way of viewing the fabric itself as having inherent worth, rather than being simply a means to an end, whether in clothing the human form or making the home beautiful and comfortable.

The concept of comfort brings us to the other side of the globe, to the western world. 'Comfort' had its source in Holland in the seventeenth century, when the increasingly prosperous Dutch artisan and merchant classes decided they wanted more than a glorified workshop in which to live. The idea that home should offer privacy and appealing surroundings for social and family activities was fed by the growing feminization of the household. Later, developments in upholstery, which were at their height in nineteenth-century France, brought the pursuit and provision of comfort to an art which was increased by engineering advances in heating and lighting.

The purposes to which we put fabric in our homes today do not vary much from those days, though the styles we choose are often very different. Our primary uses for fabric are still as window dressing (and sometimes for covering doors), on chairs and sofas as upholstery and loose covers, on other furniture such as stools and screens, and on accessories like cushions and throws. We also use fabric on our tables and our beds, on outdoor furniture in fine weather, and sometimes to cover walls, either entirely or in part.

One element of fabric which today we celebrate, but which only began to become a reality in the nineteenth century, is the brilliant abundance of colour available to us. Colour exploded with the discovery of aniline dyes in the mid- to late nineteenth century, but early versions were unreliable and destructive, fading fast and sometimes rotting the fabric. Then, in the twentieth century came new technology, the first synthetic fabrics, advancements in dyes and dyeing, and a hunger for novelty and excitement after the sad and dreary decades blighted by two world wars.

The very end of the twentieth century saw a new generation of chemically inventive fibres which combined fantastically good looks and comfort with outstanding performance and the potential for biological enhancement – carrying vitamin C or anti-bacterial agents, for example. Another, vital, late-twentieth century concern that continues today is environmental – the impact on our world and our fellow people of the cultivation and manufacture of fibres and cloth, and the drive to produce biodegradable fabrics. Recycling is a significant concern in this context – we take pleasure in reusing old linens and prints found in flea markets and elsewhere, and designers are turning to antique and vintage designs to create new, retro-inspired fabrics.

Throughout the history of fabric, its use in interiors has been closely linked to the design of clothes, never more so than in the twenty-first century. Catwalk looks, be they animal prints and faux fur, heat-responsive and body-hugging stretches or sultry satins and crushed velvets, are rapidly seen in interiors stores and catalogues. It was only a matter of time before clothes designers actually crossed the threshold of the home, tempting us not only with eminently desirable homewares but, by implication, with the corresponding lifestyle. Retailers are the new interior decorators, offering us all an entire 'look', including the fabrics that go with it, be they country house floral prints on cotton, minimalist metallic sheers, or brilliantly bohemian embroidered oriental silks. No need to employ an interior decorator – simply explore the shops.

Most notable among the international fashion designers who have become interiors retailers is Ralph Lauren. His look is instantly recognisable, as are the pure and elegant style of Nicole Farhi and the flamboyant Gianni Versace look. The interiors magazines and colour supplements have taken us right into the homes of these designers and countless others, so that we can follow their examples and the trends that they themselves have personally embraced. We know that Maria Grachvogel's voluptuous use of sequins and satin in her clothing finds a parallel in the rooms of her home, that Calvin Klein favours understatement and subtlety to the point of minimalism, and that Ralph Lauren's log cabin is a western fantasy.

This has created a paradox – we are presented with an almost bewildering variety of interiors and fashions, from which we are then expected to select what suits us in order to be our own person, with an individual style of dress and interior decoration. The result, depending on one's self-confidence and ability to resist the hype, is either freedom to be different, or confusion.

Plus ça change... In 1954, that doyen of style, Cecil Beaton, wrote in his charming volume *The Glass of Fashion* (Weidenfeld & Nicolson) that the 'purpose [of the interior decorator], like that of the couturier, has been to anticipate taste, to run before it and often create it, adjusting a pelmet of a curtain or installing an ottoman with as much authority as any Parisian dressmaker. But,' he continues with prescience, 'whereas the dressmaker can create a dress that the woman, unless she is unusually skilled, is unlikely to produce herself, the interior decorator has invaded a field that any person of taste should be able to cope with.'

Taking its lead from physical and visual texture, the aim of *Fabric: The Fired Earth Book of Natural Texture* is to celebrate, to bring alive and to help make sense of the vast range of desirable fabrics available to us today. This is not a stroll through curtain styles and sewing instructions, but an inspiringly illustrated romp through all the most beautiful and useful fabrics, the ways they can be used to best advantage, their illuminating histories and the moods they can create in our homes. Inspiration comes from interior styles and real interiors, but also from other textural sources such as the natural world and from fashion. Technological advances in the creation of fabrics by man are explained, and we look forward to future generations of people-friendly, environmentally friendly textiles that also look stunning and perform outstandingly well.

Our first chapter looks at NATURAL fabrics with soft, rough, slubby textures. Predominant among these are cottons and linens, some of which, such as ticking and other utility fabrics, and gingham, have stripes or checks. Most, however, are either plain or visually interesting on account of the weaves they employ. Herringbone, floral jacquard, twill, matelassé and seersucker are just some of the patterns and structures that result from clever weaving. We look at ways of using these fabrics to decorate our homes, and consider which interior styles (such as minimalism) best suit them.

Next come the LUXURIOUS fabrics, the warm, embracing look and feel of velvet and tweed, mohair and suede, tartan and men's suitings, brocades and tapestries... whatever is rich and heavy and napped. These are the fabrics which remind us of the time in history when keeping out the cold was a primary consideration; today the weight and grandeur of these fabrics ensure they are always taken seriously. They make fabulous curtains and hangings because they drape so well, and also magnificent upholstery because of their durability.

TRANSLUCENT fabrics are those which veil a window or bed rather than creating a solid barrier. Voiles, nets, lace, contemporary cut-outs, organdie, muslin, chiffon, thin taffeta... these fabrics float across our windows and our homes, in tune with the latest decorating styles. They are used to create layered window treatments, romantic bed hangings and even shimmering table coverings. One of the greatest areas of innovation, these inventive fabrics sometimes appear to be made of hardly more than a few gossamer strands.

In Chapter Four, the spotlight is turned on REFLECTIVE fabrics, those which shimmer, are metallic or iridescent, or are smooth and seductive like satin and taffeta. There are two polarities of fabric in this chapter – those whose fibres have been created by man, including the latest, most exciting techno-textiles, and the most aristocratic fabric in history (still popular today), namely silk.

Fabrics which are EMBELLISHED with embroidery, beadwork or trimmings are the subject of the fifth chapter. Crewelwork has a long history, as do many forms of embroidery, appliqué and passementerie. These fabrics have always been a focus in a room's decoration, because of their tactile quality and the fact that they are so often made by hand. There is an element of craftsmanship in fabrics that are embellished. Sometimes they are made into hangings for windows or beds, often they appear as cushions, while braids and tassels bring finish, a flourish and sometimes wit to many items.

The wealth of PRINTED fabrics is explored in Chapter Six, the pages of which are a riot of pictures and prints. Though we have moved away from the serious recreation of period furnishings, we still enjoy the genres that are centuries old – toile de Jouy, provençals and chintz among them. Others are more recent, such as twentieth-century artists' prints, abstract designes, camouflage and the latest computer-generated textile imaging. How to use pattern is a theme which occupies many of us when we are planning a room's decorations.

COLOUR: SIMPLE AND EXOTIC looks at the glorious kaleidoscope of colours and patterns created by dyes like indigo and techniques such as tie-dye and ikat as well as woven pattern on fabrics from across the world and many cultures. Our final chapter, FABRIC FOR REAL, is a summary of practical information about working with and caring for fabrics such as linen, silk and antique textiles, as well as some tips and ideas for transforming fabric at home.

Our aim throughout is to inform and inspire, revealing the full potential of fabric in our homes. Fabric makes a difference – it brings comfort and a sense of warmth and embrace. It creates visual fascination by introducing vibrant patterns and colours. It enhances the mood and decorative style of a room, be it minimal, glamorous, bohemian or rustic, or any other of the countless visual idioms in the contemporary decorating repertoire. Above all, the delicious textures which fabric offers enrich our homes. This is especially true where contrasting textures are juxtaposed – rough with smooth, soft with glossy, substantial with diaphanous – and where fabric textures contrast with the surfaces of other materials such as wood, stone, glass, steel and paint. The pages of this book will lead you deep into this wonderful world of sight and touch.

m

cotto

herrin

grasses &

atelassé linen

1

g b o n e

oft wool

eaves

'Natural' is one of the most evocative words we use. It trails in its wake a great swathe of happy associations. It suggests the best, wholesomeness, the antithesis of artificiality or contrivance. It also suggests unsophisticated, relaxed sensuality. We think of long sunny days uninhibited by punctuality or appointments; we imagine floating in water; we can almost taste the finest, freshest, simplest cooking ingredients, transformed into a colourful delicacy for our delight.

In fabric terms, 'natural' implies not only quality but comfort, and a range of creamy, neutral tones which can equally well be used in the home on their own or to offset cloth of stronger, richer colours. Warm in winter and cool in summer, natural fabrics are fresh yet inviting. We also like the idea of natural fabrics, their honesty and tradition, for these are the oldest textiles in history. The textures of these natural fabrics vary widely, from chunky banana fibres which remind us of the tropical climes whence they came, to super-heavy, slubby pure linen whose white expanses are reminiscent of early morning snow-covered hills untouched by any footstep, and the taut crispness of fine-spun cotton.

What exactly are natural fabrics? Broadly speaking, natural fabrics are made from fibres that are derived either from animals or from plants. Plant, or 'cellulosic', fabrics include cotton, coir, sisal and what is known as the 'bast' group, consisting of linen, jute, ramie, hemp and banana. The best-known and most widely available of these are cotton and linen, but the others have the added appeal of rarity and attractively pronounced textures. Animal yarns include hair fabrics – wool, mohair, cashmere, horsehair and so on – and silk filaments. Glossy silk we consider in detail in Chapter Four, Reflective, while the warm and embracing fabrics made from wool and other natural hairs have their place in Chapter Two, Luxurious.

Linen, cotton and the other natural fibres accord well with the pared-down mood of contemporary

decorating, whether the idiom is shabby chic or Wild West, pretty and feminine or smartly tailored. Above all, natural fibres and fabrics are at home with minimalism and its more relaxed and colourful cousin, post-minimalism. These are interior styles spawned by Modernism (also known as the International Style) and the Japanese aesthetic, embracing freedom from possessions and a yearning for simplicity and visual purity. The kings of international minimalism are John Pawson and Claudio Silvestro. In their interiors, one is aware of space and light, the geometric forms of architectural elements and furniture, the colour and texture of surfaces. There is little furniture, and what there is has clean undecorated lines and planes with virtually no ornamentation. Minimalist colours are muted, consisting almost exclusively of white, neutrals, black, matt silver and the natural colours of construction materials. In this context, what little fabric there is – on the bed, on a sofa, in a few wide panels at the window – has added significance because its rarity makes it a focus for attention, and because it offers the only fluidity, the only touch of sensual softness. The finest natural fabrics fit perfectly into the minimal interior. Post-minimalism is not as disciplined as minimalism and embraces colour warmly, in greater or smaller quantities, while adhering to the same clean lines and relative lack of clutter.

At our windows, natural fabrics need little elaboration to show their best qualities. Roman blinds are handsome, with the right unfussy, tailored look. Contemporary curtains either hang in completely flat panels or are barely gathered on a rod or wire, using clips or tabs, or with the top of the curtain pierced by eyelets. Long curtains drape on the floor, their length enlivened with panels of contrasting colour or texture at the sides, bottom or top, or even across the middle. Loose covers with simple, clean lines can be pressed and stretched to give sofas and chairs a sharp finish, or be purposely scrunched up while damp to give them added tactile quality once back on the furniture.

Regardless of the style of your home, natural fabrics can be used for every purpose for which fabric is required, from simple curtain treatments to upholstery, loose covers and accessories, and everyday napkins and the cloths with which we dry glass or mop up in the kitchen – each use depending on the fabric's weight, strength and absorbency, and the fineness of its texture. Upholstery fabrics need to be the strongest and most hardwearing, but that doesn't mean their texture is always shaggy or craggy. On the contrary, some of the best are meltingly smooth – from fine damask to glossy linen mixes. You can even use natural fabrics on the floor – apart from laying rugs, you can make a floor covering with cotton canvas, priming it and laying on patterned layers of paint then coating it with varnish to transform it into a traditional floorcloth.

On our beds, sheets made of pure linen offer the ultimate in practicality and sensuality, especially when they bring to the bedroom the unmistakable snap of fresh country air from having been dried outdoors on a washing line in the sun – what could be more luxurious? Linen is non-allergic and antistatic, and is also able to absorb nearly one-fifth of its weight in moisture, further qualities which make it ideal for bed sheeting and pillowcases. At the dining table, the quickest way to introduce a sense of occasion is to dress it in linen or cotton. Being absorbent and washing well, both fabrics make ideal table linen. But be warned – once you are addicted to linen napkins and bedding, nothing else will do. Napkins and pillowcases are, after all, among the few fabric items ever to touch the delicate skin of your face, so it is natural to want the best.

The outdoor life is well suited to linen and cotton, either intentionally or by default. A cushion, be it floral or striped, bright or pale, that has given good service indoors but has become faded or outdated finds a new existence on the lawn or on an old wicker chair. An aged curtain is transformed into an outdoor tablecloth or even (if it is still tough enough) made into

seats and backs for folding garden furniture such as directors' chairs and deckchairs. In contrast, new bright colours and patterns bring life into the garden on the later summer months when vegetation is a little tired and dusty, and on fine days in spring and autumn. In warmer regions hot colours match the climate, while neutrals introduce a contrasting cool visual element.

Cotton and linen checks and stripes never go out of fashion – they are always fresh and young. They satisfy some part of our nature in the same way as the rhythm of furrows on a ploughed field or the fenestration on shiny new buildings. The latest generation of stripes incorporates rainbow colours, jumbled up in a vibrant clash of red, yellow, green and blue, the stripes sometimes neatly regular as in the past, sometimes of seemingly random widths and spacings, like a barcode. While looking uncompromisingly contemporary, multicoloured striped designs like these crop up in the history of fabric, notably in the creations of the weaving workshop of the influential Bauhaus in Weimar and Dessau in the 1920s and early '30s. Of all the workshops in the Bauhaus, this was the one that was a commercial success, selling rugs and fabric for modern interiors. Gunte Stölzl was an outstanding student and teacher at the Bauhaus, and her textile designs have rightly been the focus of enthusiastic attention in recent years. One of her rug designs has recently been recreated by retailer Christopher Farr. Anni Albers, another member of the workshop, described how they cast aside historical influences and returned to first principles to create fresh designs: 'this play with materials produced amazing results, textiles striking in their novelty, their fullness of colour and texture, and possessing often a quite barbaric beauty.'

Like stripes, checks are timeless, none more so than unsophisticated gingham. 'Gingham' once referred to an entire family of fabrics including plaids and stripes, but now we use it to mean a fabric with horizontal and vertical stripes of one colour and equal width, often in red, blue or brown on a white or neutral ground. These **crossing stripes** produce the reassuringly familiar simple check. Today gingham comes in a variety of weights and pattern sizes for different uses. The lightest-weight, finely checked gingham is akin to a voile floating at the window, while the heaviest will withstand the wear to which upholstery is subjected.

Amongst the classic stripes is puckered **seersucker**, which has the added attraction of supreme practicality. (You never need to iron it.) Tough cotton canvas with cheerful stripes is ideal for deckchairs and outdoor furniture. While we relish the origins of some traditional striped and checked **patterns**, such as the blue-and-white striped fabric used for butchers' aprons and mattress ticking, nonetheless today we love these fabrics for themselves. Originally destined for specific and hard use by tradesmen and other working people, these checked and striped fabrics today come under the umbrella term 'utility fabrics'. They are widely available, **hardwearing** (they were, after all, 'working' fabrics), versatile and popular. Like all checks and stripes, they are useful for covering sofas, tables, cushions and beds, or as curtains, and they complement both contemporary furniture and country antiques.

Checks and stripes are also a traditional element in compiling a sophisticated Swedish or **continental look**, combined with toile de Jouy or florals. The straight lines and freshness of stripes and checks balance the elaborate designs of these other fabrics and prevent them from becoming overbearing. Use a **toile** on the walls of a sitting room or bedroom, for example, stretched between battens screwed into the plaster. Add a medium- or large-scale check on the sofa or bed, then cover chairs and stools with stripes – all in the same colour on white or neutral. In a dining room or kitchen, use a floral or toile fabric to cover the table (a busy design helps disguise the odd spill), with checked or striped table napkins and contrasting squab cushions for

the chair seats in the same tonal range. Solid wooden furniture that is blond, polished or painted goes well with these **decorative** schemes. Being fresh and smart, this style of mixing checks and stripes with other patterns has found favour across the world – in the bedroom of diplomat and decorator Jaime Parladé's conciergerie in the Lot in France, for example, where the tones are washed-out blues and reds and the patterns even include an original William Morris floral textile. Elsewhere, the style can be seen in a bedroom decorated by Barry Dixon for a house in Virginia, where the browns of a toile showing oriental scenes set the tone for a variety of woven and printed patterns around the room. Even the carpet is a plaid in tones of cream and soft greyish-brown.

Fabrics which are striped and checked can be two-tone (usually one colour with white or cream, or two shades of the same colour), multicoloured or 'self-coloured'. 'Self-coloured' means that the yarn which makes up the **threads** in both warp (which runs continuously down the cloth) and weft (which runs from side to side of the cloth on the loom and on the roll) is all of one colour. The pattern is the result of the intervals at which the threads go over and under each other – in other words, the pattern is created by the **weave** and thereby also adds texture. Self-coloured fabrics in white and neutrals such as grey, taupe and cream are the epitome of discretion and are especially suited to furnishing low-key, unfussy minimalist and Modernist style interiors. In the immaculate, empty, serene interior of a building designed by John Pawson, subtle changes in **texture** are all the more important. In this context, natural fabrics in pale colours do not draw attention to themselves, but their solid quality and the texture of their woven pattern appeals both visually and to the touch. Self-coloured fabrics in brighter colours, such as tomato and pea green, are also at home in the post-minimalist interior, which is much less restrained in its use of bright colour and playful decorative details.

There are countless different weaves available to the fabric designer, many of them geometric (stripes, herringbone and small repeat patterns, for example), while others are florid or floral. The former are made on a simple 'dobby' loom, while the latter have their origins in the invention of the Jacquard loom, which allows patterns both small and large to be woven into the substance of the cloth. Small dobby patterns often consist of a tiny star or motif repeated regularly across the cloth. Large, bold and often detailed Jacquard patterns repeating across the cloth, usually incorporating floral and leafy forms, are known as damasks. Traditionally, damask is reversible, with its woven pattern accentuated by areas of glossy satin weave. Damasks create a sophisticated, sumptuous mood when used to furnish an interior. They go well with dark wood antique furniture, with gilding on furniture and picture frames, with intricately patterned Persian rugs, and with deep colours such as burgundy red, Lincoln green, bitter chocolate brown and even black.

Joseph-Marie Jacquard (1752–1834) was the son of a silk master living in Lyons, who employed his young son's labour in operating the loom strings – a numbingly tedious business. Jacquard's first attempt at designing an advanced loom was useful only for weaving fishing nets; in 1801 (improved in 1804), however, he brought together and modified the inventions of two other men for moving needles and using a perforated card to guide them. As a result, complex and detailed designs could be woven into the cloth, the pattern dictated by which warp threads were raised and which dropped each time the shuttle moved the weft across the loom. The Jacquard loom is still very much in use today, in a thundering, computer-controlled, rapier-shuttled form found in textile mills across the world.

A form of Jacquard-woven cotton which combines woven pattern with particularly pronounced texture is matelassé. This is a form of 'doublecloth', a substantial, reversible fabric constructed rather as if two lighter cloths had been woven together. Matelassé has the added interest of appearing to be quilted or embossed, an effect achieved by the insertion of an extra, coarser yarn into the weft. It makes charming, nostalgic bed covers and curtains, but though substantial is not generally suitable for upholstery as the raised parts are vulnerable to wear.

Linen and cotton are the most prominent of the natural fabrics. Linen is probably the first fibre that humankind learnt to weave – it is said to pre-date the wheel. The Egyptians wrapped mummies in it and the Book of Genesis in the Bible mentions it, as does St Matthew's Gospel. The Phoenicians and Greeks used it, and the Romans grew it in various parts of their Empire. Everywhere it was a status symbol. It was considered the purest fibre for the making of altar cloths, and its use spread with Christianity. Linen was accepted by many abbeys in Europe as a tithe or rental payment from their tenants. St Patrick, the patron saint of Ireland, is said to have been buried in a shroud of pure Irish linen. Ireland, together with Flanders on the European mainland, is the place above all that is associated with fine linen cloth because of its cultivation of the crop over the centuries, the part it has played in its economic history, and the high quality of the cloth that it produces today. Much of this is exported to the United States, a trade which dates significantly from 1704 when the duty on Irish linens exported into the American colonies was lifted. (At one time, later in the eighteenth century, Irish farmers in turn imported flax seed from America, their own having proved insufficiently productive.) Just as the choice of fabrics and textures we can use to decorate our homes today is the result to a large extent of trends in the retail market, so in the past the availability and use of fabrics was closely tied up with world trade. Fabrics from afar have always been coveted as a luxury, bringing prestige into our homes.

Like silk, linen is an astonishing fibre that comes almost readymade from nature. Long threads of linen are present in the outer cortex of the plant's stems as it grows in the fields. *Linum usitatissimum* is a 'hundred-day' crop, harvested roughly a hundred days after being sown. Some of the stages required to transform it into the fabric that we love are called 'retting' (softening the plant in water), 'scutching' (beating the woody core of the plant's stem away from the fibres) and 'hackling' (combing the fibres straight and smooth). Depending on its final use, the linen yarn is spun then twisted, polished or otherwise finished, bleached or dyed. The various finishing techniques give us linen with a wide variety of looks and 'handles', from canvas-like, slubby textures to the polish of a heavy damask tablecloth and the finest lightweight fabric for window dressing and for the fashion industry, where linen is equally popular. The most recent development is a finish which reduces linen's famous propensity for creasing and crushing.

The story of cotton is, in geographic terms, a triangular one; in political terms it is dramatic, involving as it does wars, Empire, slavery and the emergence of the contemporary world's great super-power. The three points on the globe most closely associated with the history of cotton are India, Britain and what is now the USA. Britain, once a great cotton manufacturer, has fallen by the wayside but cotton is still significant in the USA and India. In India the cultivation and processing of around eighty different varieties of cotton account for over a fifth of the country's industrial production, employing around fifteen million people.

India, along with Central and South America, was one of the first places where cotton was cultivated and cloth created from it, thousands of years ago. As the British spread their trading links across the subcontinent in the late sixteenth and early seventeenth centuries, they saw the finest of these fabrics at the Moghul courts. At first they bought them because they were popular in Holland, and the British wanted spices from the Dutch-held East Indies. But by the middle of the

seventeenth century Indian patterned fabrics were being imported into Britain for their own sake, from the port of Calicut (hence 'calico', a type of cotton specked with brown seeds). This caused controversy because cotton was seen by some as a threat to the indigenous woollen industry. The raw material was still imported into Britain, however, to feed the growing cotton manufacturing industry. Cotton cloth was then exported back to India on terms favourable to the seat of Empire, a perceived iniquity which later gave rise to Mahatma Ghandi's famous 'homespun' campaign of non-violent resistance to rule by the British Raj. He urged Indians to wear only cloth made locally, effectively boycotting British-made cotton cloth.

Meanwhile, in the American South the cotton industry was conceived from the start as a large-scale, money-making enterprise. Plantation owners with great tracts of land and slaves to work it looked for suitable crops. These included indigo (more about this in Chapter Seven, Colour: Simple and Exotic), rice, tobacco... and cotton. In the northern states, too, entrepreneurs found cotton appealing.

In harvesting the cotton crop the task which was slowest and most laborious, consuming the energies of large numbers of slaves in the southern states, was that of separating the seed from the fluff, by hand or by the inefficient 'bowing' method. This problem was solved by an invention of the young Eli Whitney, who sauntered into the story in 1792 after graduating from Yale. Visiting friends in Savannah, he noticed this difficulty and promptly introduced a mechanical device for quick and efficient deseeding, using two contra-rotating drums (an idea rediscovered for washing machines in the twenty-first century by the inventor James Dyson).

By the early nineteenth century, cotton fabrics had taken the place of woollens as the fashionable choice for decorating interiors in England and New England alike, except in the more masculine domains of the library and dining room where wool and sometimes silk were favoured. For bed hangings, upholstery and window treatments, cotton was increasingly **popular** and 'cases' (the loose covers laid over upholstered furniture on all but the smartest occasions) were always cotton or linen because these washed well.

In the modern age and with our concern for the environmental impact of the materials we consume in our daily lives, it is not possible to overlook the fact that cotton production has caused concern. Great swathes of the American South have been laid waste by intensive farming methods. Compared with synthetic fibres, which can be made in a factory close to centres of consumption, cotton needs large areas in which to grow and has a high mileage environmental price tag as it crosses the globe to its final destination in our homes. There is some hope in **organic**, chemical-free production projects but, in the words of an ecologist quoted in the *National Geographic* magazine in June 1994, 'Probably, if we were **environmentally sensitive**, we would [use] polyester.' Among the most exciting developments in cotton is the work of Sally Fox in Texas. She is propagating plants whose cotton is **naturally coloured** – whole fields of rusty brown, leafy green or dusty blue which, when spun and woven into cloth, obviate the necessity for polluting bleaches and dyes. Perhaps most extraordinary of all, fabric made from such naturally coloured cloth does not fade – the colours apparently deepen with washing.

Other, often more fragile textiles such as those made from banana and pineapple leaves and fronds offer wonderfully inviting textures for use in our homes. Sometimes **matt**, sometimes **glossy**, their texture always makes one want to reach out and touch. Whether plaited and coiled into great floor cushions or woven into springy textiles to cover cushions and chairs, their rugged looks and shades of brown fit perfectly into the **modern rustic** look. Modern rustic combines wicker baskets and roaring log fires with the clean lines

of contemporary and country furniture and accessories, colour and texture being always to the fore. Some brittle plant-leaf **fibres** are sold already backed with fabric made from other, often manmade, fibres to lend them added strength and longevity.

Paper is another fibre used increasingly in fashion and interiors (Reiko Sudo's fabrics incorporating shredded paper are a fine example), and also in flooring. The finest paper often, in turn, contains cotton or linen fibres. In yet another turn, paper can be formed to look like **raffia** or hemp which is then woven into cloth. An example of this, made by Bruno Triplet, is backed with a film of PVC in order to make it sufficiently tough to be used to upholster dining chairs and other small pieces of furniture. In the Japanese idiom, the matt, milky finish of finely milled **paper** is framed by wooden sliding screens used to divide one area in the home from another and from passageways, an elegant but not soundproof device for organizing space.

Some natural fabrics may shrink, fade, become brittle over time or need ironing, but these qualities are all part of their known charm and don't stop us loving them. In spite of the wonderful advances in the creation of fibres invented or engineered by mankind, the beauty, fabulous **textures**, and comeliness of natural fabrics will never be eclipsed – far from it. Natural fabrics have a natural **allure**. In the home of the future, there will surely be room for both.

velvet

tweed

cashm

tapestry

leather

mohair
e k e
artan
& suede

'The most sensu
delight the skin
wool... and moha
others, are trie
pleasure zones.'

al fabrics
 Cashmere,
ir velvet among
d and tested

Ilse Crawford

Luxurious fabrics are the most outstandingly sensual. Touch the astonishing fluid softness of alpaca or cashmere and be uplifted. The pliant warmth of velvet pile feels as soft and supple as the coat of a favourite hound. The embrace of faux fur induces a shiver of delight. Cuddly wool has many manifestations – simple, substantial, plain-weave woollens that are heavy and fall beautifully; hirsute tweed with a manly robustness to the touch which also carries echoes of fresh air and countryside; sophisticated restrained worsteds and suiting fabrics with an understated tensile strength and smooth style. These fabrics are superb. Their luxury cushions and absorbs us. They bring an aura of extravagance into our homes, even if used in small quantities – a fluffy throw or a velvet cushion.

Velvet, cashmere, pashmina, leather, tapestry, brocade, chenille, tartan, tweed, woollen suitings... of all the fabrics in this book, these are the noble families, the ones with lineage and gravitas, with history and tradition behind them, the ones which are substantial and serious. Their ancestry can be traced back over the centuries, and that's important to them, and us. Generally expensive, not to be embarked upon lightly, and not easy to work with for the inexperienced, they bring with them into your home an air of distinction. These classics are reassuring, a reminder that, however ingenious and enticing the latest fibres invented by man, traditional quality holds firm.

There are, however, some amongst the clever new manmade fabrics which fall happily into the luxurious category. This latest generation has breeding and a likeness to their aristocratic forebears without their superior manner. Fabrics such as fake fur, matt faux suedes and leathers (some of them, astonishingly, machine-washable), fleece and cotton jersey embrace and pamper us. Soft and supple, they are fabrics to wallow in, lie back against or wrap around us on sofas and in deep armchairs, and to use on or in our beds.

Visually, luxurious fabrics are a feast. They have texture in abundance, both to look at and to feel. They have a depth of colour, sometimes enhanced by pile, that draws the eye inwards. Colours are often rich and sonorous, occasionally incorporating gold and silver threads. Some of the younger scions of the family, meanwhile, display disobedient disregard for their forebears in adopting more vibrant tones which are appealing for being fresh and bright – faux suede in brilliant shades of pink and green, for example, and metallic faux leather in purple or silver. In other words, the traditional rich tonal range has been joined by more dynamic and playful shades which find their natural home in today's post-minimalist (pared-down but colourful) contemporary interiors.

While some luxurious fabrics are instantly at home with antique furniture and the scent of beeswax, others accord well with the emphasis in contemporary decorating on contrasts in texture as much as on the more conventional yardsticks of colour and pattern. Black leather has an impeccable Modernist pedigree, contrasted with gleaming chrome on furniture inspired by the curvaceous designs of Eileen Gray and Charlotte Perriand. Snow-white leather and velvet are the ultimate, ostentatiously luxurious textiles in the contemporary repertoire – the more so for being impractical. These and other more accessible and easy-care modern fabrics, such as grey fleece and faux suedes in muted tones, are as much in keeping with minimalist simplicity in an interior as with gilded, glossy glamour.

The luxurious fabrics have a further distinction – they remind us of days when the two primary functions of textiles, in northern climes at least, both in clothing and in the home, were to express status and to exclude cold. The finest silk brocatelle was for wealthy, powerful families and royalty; tapestries hung on the walls told stories of valour while attempting to keep at bay the relentless chill of winter. Today's homes are, mostly, a world away from this scenario. We are fortunate to be able to take double glazing and central heating for granted, which leaves us free to enjoy luxurious fabrics for themselves. We revel in their appearance, their texture and colour, and their reassuring sense of warmth and history, free from the practical necessity of keeping out draughts.

Designers across the world love to work with the finest fabrics, but the reputations of some positively rest on their use of the aristocrats of the textile world, both antique and modern. Alberto Pinto is one such, his opulent interiors glowing with richly coloured velvet and brocade at windows, on walls, on furniture and alongside gilded wood, glittering chandeliers and antique paintings. Alidad is famous for his rooms encrusted with texture and aglow with colour and pattern, much of it Islamic in origin. The rich, fabrics on the furniture in his own apartment (often fragments of woollen kilims) are set against a backdrop of equally fabulous colour and pattern on the walls and ceilings of his rooms. At the opposite end of the luxurious spectrum is Jenny Armit, whose style can be described as modern classic, incorporating furniture and the finest fabrics by the best contemporary designers. Her interiors can be dark and sumptuous or cool and airy.

Modern luxuries like fleece and faux fur are sufficiently fluid to be made into bed covers, beanbag covers, throws and other accessories, as are traditional corduroy and woollen fabrics. Soft leather and suede cover seating cubes (which can also be used as occasional tables). Otherwise, most of the fabrics in this chapter are substantial and tend to be used for curtains and upholstery. Some are not suitable for upholstery, however. The pile on velvet, for example, can look shabby quite quickly on the seat of a chair where it receives regular use. There are other ways of using velvet – for example, on the walls, covering upholstered padded squares or rectangles, in a contemporary form of panelling. Leather panels can be used in this way too. Here is an opportunity for colour mixing, each

panel on the wall being a different colour, or two or three colours jumbled together seemingly at random. In a position where the panels are likely to be subjected to contact and friction, such as across the head of a bed, leather is the ideal alternative to velvet for covering padded panels. It is more resilient, has no pile to be disturbed, and can be polished up if it shows unwelcome signs of wear. On furniture, however, the patina of age is part of leather's charm.

Velvet is nonetheless probably the most popular and accessible of the luxury fabrics, and certainly the most famous of the pile fabrics. Its lovely texture and the depth and variations in the colour on its piled surface as the light falls on its folds make velvet welcome in any smart interior, be it post-minimalist or grand country house style. When thoroughly battered and worn with age, and possibly faded in stripes where it has been bleached by the sun, velvet even has a place in a bohemian sitting room or a country kitchen.

The pile on velvet, like that on a carpet, is formed by the upstanding tufts which give it a pronounced third dimension. This pile is produced on the loom by a third thread, in addition to the warp and weft and kept in place by them. Traditionally, this third thread was woven looped over metal wires, along which it was cut to form the pile. Today this method is only used for the finest, exorbitantly expensive silk velvet for historic houses and connoisseurs. Most velvet is now made from other fibres, notably cotton or viscose, and by the 'face-to-face' method. This means that instead of looping over a wire, the third thread continues across to another cloth which is being woven at the same time as the first on the same loom. A fast-moving blade then slices horizontally between the two cloths, separating them. The two lengths of velvet, which had been face to face, are wound away on to different rolls.

Finished velvet can be printed, woven in wide stripes with flat-weave intervals, or crushed for added decorative effect. To the velvet manufacturer who has put so much effort into preserving and enhancing the smooth, regular, glossy pile of a length of **fine velvet**, the process of crushing or double-crushing velvet is bizarre. Lengths of otherwise finished fabric are dampened, unravelled and crammed into a wooden chest where they are twice pummelled relentlessly by heavy rams. The result is muted and tactile and gives the fabric an **aura of age**. Double-crushed velvet looks good surrounded by polished wooden floors, leather armchairs, an open fire in the grate and ancestral paintings on the walls.

The most exclusive velvets are Genoa, Utrecht and figured cloths. Genoa velvets have a multicoloured pile which may be cut or uncut. Utrecht velvet has a pattern **embossed** into it using etched and heated metal rollers. Figured velvet only has pile in the places where the pattern demands it; elsewhere the pile is woven back into the background fabric. All these three types of velvet are enormously **expensive** but are incomparably effective.

Velvet is not only a historic fabric – like any other, it is open to re-interpretation or re-invention for the contemporary age. The latest intriguing **velvets** are made from polyester for a harder, shinier finish but a wonderfully supple and hardwearing cloth, or from linen for a rumpled, slubby, matt effect. The most delightful new velvets, incontrovertibly **glamorous**, are those which incorporate in their piles a nylon fibre, wider or thinner, which gives a delicious glitter to the fabric. A coarser nylon fibre – which on close examination looks like a piece of narrow, clear plastic tape – gives a more obvious reflection, while an ultra-fine ribbon of nylon, almost a thread, gives a subtle, sophisticated sparkle. This velvet lends a magical and **seductive** touch to curtains and covers in a bedroom or other inner sanctuary, or indeed in any room that is often in use after dark, as if stardust had been scattered over them.

Besides velvet, other less exclusive pile fabrics include **corduroy** (which has ribs of pile between plain-weave stripes), velour (a densely woven, hardwearing fabric with a shallow pile, useful for upholstery), towelling and uncut **moquette**. The pile on this moquette is looped and left looped (hence 'uncut'). This is the toughest pile fabric, now largely used for the upholstery on seating in halls and hotels rather than in our homes, where its practical, good-looking qualities come into their own. The other fabrics in this group are useful around the home for covering beanbags and cushions, for curtains and bed covers, but are not ideal for tablecloths – smooth, pile-free fabrics are more **practical** here.

Of the warm, luxurious fibres, wool is the one that has probably been in use for longer than any other. **Wool** is a complex protein, resilient, elastic and wavy. It is an astonishing fibre, able to be bent 30,000 times and stretched up to one-third of its length without being damaged. Its structure, with an inner cortex and outer layer of overlapping scales, allows it to absorb evaporated water but repel actual liquids. The earliest known woollen cloth was excavated in Denmark and dated to around 1500 BC, but the use of wool is believed to be much older, possibly dating to 9000 BC. Spinning was at first by hand, then by spinning wheel, while **looms** for weaving cloth from the yarn are thought to have been invented around 2000 BC.

For many centuries, and possibly millennia, it has been appreciated that different breeds of sheep produce different wool suitable for different end uses. **Fleece** from the Exmoor Horn, for example, is traditionally used to create the finest smooth woollen cloth, such as the green baize which when laid over slate creates the surface of billiard tables. The wool from Lincoln and Leicester breeds is famously long and **lustrous**. The Merino breed, whose soft wool is mostly used to make worsteds and **knitwear**, including knitted throws, was imported from Spain into Australia where it contributed to establishing that country's vast sheep-rearing industry. Cheviot sheep give wool for tweed. Other, tougher and hardwearing wools like Black-faced Highland are favoured for making carpets.

The finest, smoothest yarn is known as 'worsted', the name also given to the cloth woven from it, which is likewise smooth and flat with none of the hairiness we associate with woollen fabrics like tweed. The reason why worsted is so strong, supple and smooth is that it is made from the very best wool and is combed before spinning. Long fibres are heated and rolled to reduce the natural crimp, then laid parallel by various processes before being twisted. The result is a yarn with an almost perfectly round profile, and a fabulous cloth which is expensive but long-lasting. Top-quality suitings are generally worsteds. No longer only confined to being worn on one's back, they include sombre and discreet variations on the stripe and check, such as pinstripe (the finest pale stripe on a dark background), chalkstripe (a thicker pale stripe), and Prince of Wales, houndstooth and dogtooth checks (different scales of check resulting in a small, spiky, lozenge-shaped pattern on the cloth). Because of the popularity of using suitings in interiors, some furnishing fabrics are now made with weaves which imitate the traditional suiting patterns, but are intended only for use in the home.

Others in the range of woollen fabrics originally designed for clothing are wool flannel, a soft, warm plain weave that is usually grey, and tweed. Both flannel and tweed are 'twill' weaves, created by a diagonal movement of the pattern of warp and weft threads as the cloth is formed on the loom. Tweeds and flannel make fine curtains, throws, bed covers and cushions, but aren't always suitable for upholstery and may be scratchy to the touch. A worsted suiting fabric is smooth and would withstand the wear for upholstery.

The use of any of these fabrics in an interior brings not only physical warmth and luxury from the wool

content of the cloth, but also a touch of wit and irreverence because they have apparently been taken out of context. The rich browns and greys so often seen in them are once again popular for decorating interiors. Using men's suiting fabrics (and fabrics designed to look like them) for upholstery is not, however, an entirely new idea. In the United States in the middle of the nineteenth century, many regions in rural states were inaccessible to tradesmen, and good-quality cloth was hard to come by. When you had some, you used it for whatever purposes were currently required, so that substantial men's suiting fabric like worsted soon found its way on to upholstered furniture.

Two other perennial patterns traditionally manifested in wool cloth are tartan and paisley. Paisley is a pattern of repeating and elaborated curving teardrop shapes found in many cultures (the Persian *boteh*, for example). Tartan is inevitably associated with Scotland, where different patterns in different combinations of colours are linked to the various historic families or clans, and to their activities. Before the nineteenth century, however, 'tartan' meant simply a closely woven cloth made from Highland sheep wool, which was of a fine, hard staple. Queen Victoria and Prince Albert popularized tartan, helped by pictures of the redecoration of Balmoral Castle, completed in 1855, in which it was heavily applied. Victorian 'improvers' regularized these romanticized tartan patterns, introducing new colours (most notably dark greens and blues) and publishing the tartans in books. The myth was established and became fact.

Today, tartans or 'plaids' appear in every colour available, in fabric made from every type of fibre. Tartan has been set free for use on almost any conceivable surface in the home, should you want it – on curtains, loose covers and upholstery, on accessories such as cushions, on fabric to cover walls and ceilings, and on carpets to cover floors. Tablemats, china and table linen, bedlinen, even candles have tartan printed on them or woven into them. Copious use of strongly coloured tartan results in a powerful, imposing, essentially masculine look which, with the addition of heavy wooden furniture or items made from antlers, is positively baronial. Used with a lighter touch – a single wool tartan rug thrown over a faded chair or the back of a sofa, or folded at the foot of a guest bed, for example – tartan is friendly and familiar. Some tartans, such as those with a pale or red background, would even be at home in a more feminine decorative scheme alongside white or neutral fabrics, or an eclectic mix of lightweight patterns.

Traditionally wool, as well as linen and silk, was woven into patterned damask using the Jacquard loom. Brocade is formed on the loom in the same way as damask but has a raised pattern in additional colours, created by the introduction of extra, non-structural threads which float behind the fabric when not needed. Tapestry is similar to brocade in having a pronounced texture, but different in that all the colours needed to create patterns and pictures are there in the threads of warp and weft. When required by the design, a colour is brought to the surface but otherwise it floats or is woven in across the back of the fabric, out of sight.

Originally, wool tapestry was handmade on a loom, the intention being to imitate hand-stitched needlework. Some early tapestry designs were related to the intricate and elaborate illuminations in religious books created in the monasteries. Heraldic motifs were incorporated and can be seen on the oldest known tapestry, the Cloth of St Géréon, dating from the early eleventh century. Woven in seven colours, fragments of this are now preserved in various museums across Europe, including the Victoria & Albert Museum in London and the Musée Historique des Tissus in Lyon, France.

In the Middle Ages, many countries produced tapestries destined to hang in the castles of their churchmen, noblemen and rulers, showing scenes from history,

mythology and the Bible, and these were carried with them when they moved from one abode to another. By the end of the fourteenth century certain places had become important centres for creating these textiles, namely Brussels, Arras, Tournai and Flanders. Later Aubusson emerged as a great manufactory, King Henri IV having closed French borders in 1601 to tapestries made abroad. By the end of the eighteenth century, panelling and wallpaper had taken over as fashionable wallcoverings, and the luxury business of making individual tapestries finally all but disappeared with the upheavals across Europe, most notably the French Revolution. William Morris in the nineteenth century revived tapestry-making under the principles of the Arts and Crafts Movement (parallel to the Mission Movement in America), calling it 'the noblest of all the arts of weaving'. With the Industrial Revolution machine-made tapestry fabric became possible. It has proved lastingly popular for upholstery, the rigours of which its structure is well suited to withstand, over the whole range of smart interior styles.

Fabrics with pronounced texture, such as bouclé and chenille, are created by using fancy yarns. Bouclé has a yarn in which one thread is longer than the other, and bobbles out from it in curls and twists. Chenille is an interesting yarn which consists of three threads. Traditionally, it is made from weaving a fabric that is then cut into strips horizontally; the severed warp threads stick out all round, giving a deep, rumpled texture which transfers to the cloth. Another textured yarn, gimp, is a spiral yarn consisting of two threads twisting in opposite directions, with a third forming loops. In any of these yarns, one thread of slightly different or contrasting colour adds visual texture to the finished fabric. As with all fabrics, the use to which you put textiles formed from these yarns depends to a large extent on their strength – almost any fabric will make curtains but few are sufficiently hardwearing for upholstery. Your supplier will advise you on cloths. Recycling of textiles is an issue of increasing concern to us all. If it is not recycled, waste from the manufacturing process and the items we no longer want for whatever reason end up in the earth in landfill sites or are burnt. Governments, industry and individuals are engaged in reducing waste at every stage. But the recycling of woollen fabrics is nothing new. There is a whole tribe of what were once known as 're-manufactured' wools. These included 'shoddy', a yarn made from unravelled knitwear and tweed, and 'mungo', in which short fibres obtained from felt and worsteds were blended with new cotton or wool to make a coarse yarn. The latest recycled fabrics include woollens like the 'reSKU' range by Interface Fabrics, a collection of pleasing small woven patterns for upholstery whose tonal range is dictated by the existing colour of the recycled fibres – no further dyeing takes place. This company also makes luxurious fabrics formed from spun recycled polyester that had a previous life in the form of plastic bottles. A trend for making cushion covers from old woollen jumpers, sometimes boiled and felted first, can also be described as an inventive form of recycling. Squares or other shapes of this cloth can be joined together into blankets or throws as in patchwork, which is, after all, a venerable and long-lived system for preventing waste.

Sheep's wool is not, of course, the only animal fibre used for making fabric. Other animals include horses (horsehair or hair cloth), goats (mohair, cashmere, pashmina), camels (camel hair, vicuna, guanaco), the llama and the alpaca. Alpaca hair is extremely soft and fine, while llama is a mixture of coarse and fine, usually separated for different uses. The angora goat gives us fluffy mohair, which dyes particularly well, and cashmere, the finest, softest fibres of which each animal yields only about half a pound a year. Pashmina is the exquisitely fine hair from the belly of the Himalayan mountain goat. The latest variation on cashmere is 'cashgora', a blend with angora, the hair of the angora rabbit, fine, fluffy and slippery. Vicuna is a small member of the camel family that lives high in the Andes and

gives us possibly the rarest (certainly among the most expensive) and softest of animal fibres. Guanaco hair is downy, guanaquito being the pelt of the baby guanaco when it is about a week old.

All these fibres are expensive, some so much so that their use is hardly realistic unless they are blended with silk, wool and manmade or other fibres. We are also now more aware of ecological issues relating to them. Nonetheless, these exclusive alternatives to warming woollen cloth are amongst the most sublime of the luxurious fabrics, giving us textures of seductive tenderness. Their high financial cost means that we are most likely to use fabrics incorporating these fibres in small quantities, as cushions and throws, which we can actually snuggle up to. Their softness can be emphasized by a contrasting textured fabric used alongside as a wide, flat border to a throw, for example, or to back a cushion. This contrasting fabric could be a slippery satin or a matt, slubby linen.

The luxurious interior is one into which we want to sink, wrapping ourselves in the sybaritic delights of heavy, soft, rich and rare fabrics. It is also an interior that has presence, either because the historical resonance of its fabrics and their regal colours confer grandeur or, in a contemporary setting, because of the superb quality and finish of its materials. In a modern home with clean lines and simple furnishings, luxurious fabrics like velvet and leather lend comfort and fluidity while retaining their aura of exclusivity. In traditional interiors, luxurious fabrics are sumptuous and serious. Luxury is a seductive quality – once enjoyed, it is not easy to renounce – and fabric is its agent in the interiors of our homes. A touch of luxury, however great or small, never goes amiss. Be the mood simple or extravagant, fabric has the power to bring texture and luxury into a room, and no fabrics achieve this as effortlessly as those that are themselves joyfully, sensually luxurious by their very nature.

organ

sheers

m

layers

die voile
uslin
of net

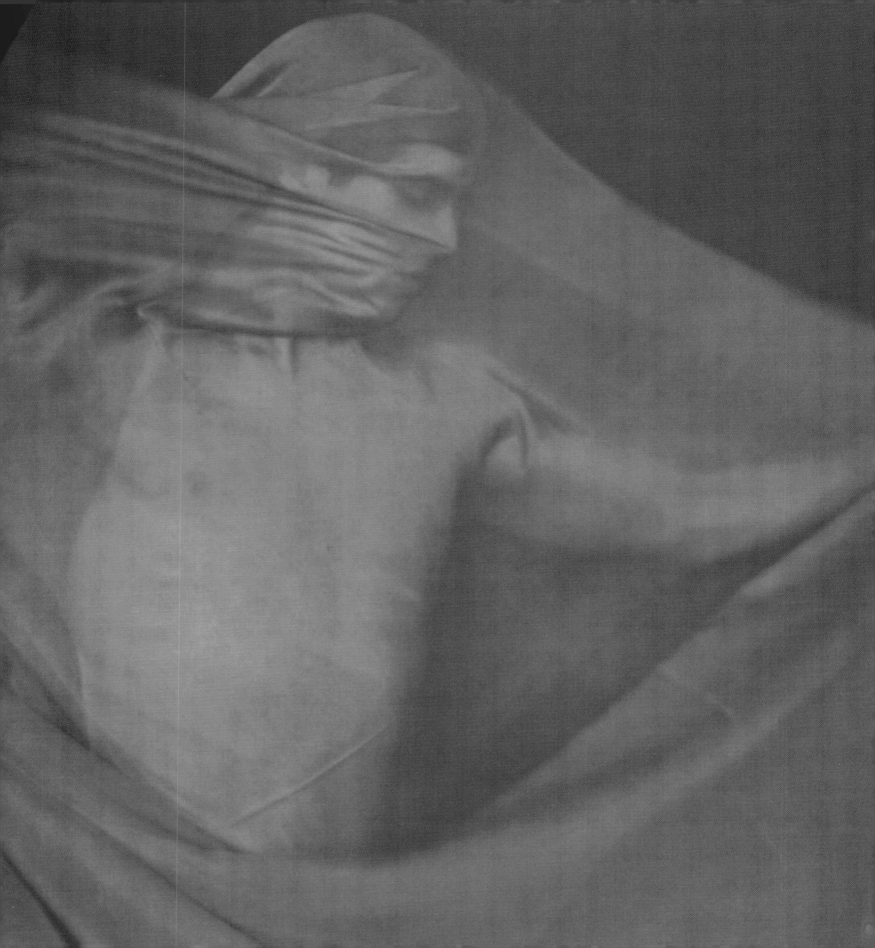

Translucent fabrics have a fragile, dreamy quality, partly because of the way that they play with light, partly simply because of their physical lack of substance. One thinks of exquisite iridescent insect wings too delicate to touch or hold, the delicious rustle of crisp tissue paper, or the fly-away fairy lanterns that hold the precious seeds of cottage plants long after summer has faded into autumn. To the touch, the texture of these fabrics is sometimes smooth and filmy, sometimes rough. Lightness both in weight and in degree of transparency defines the translucent fabrics. Airiness and playfulness characterize these ethereal beauties.

Translucents filter light, they cast sensual shadows, they are enticing; they alter our perceptions. They invite us to look through, look beyond. The contrast between the heavy, luxurious textiles in the previous chapter and the light, floaty fabrics we look at in this chapter could not be greater. Whereas those fabrics are substantial, serious and solid, translucents are insubstantial, often humorous and delightful. The velvets and woollens in the previous chapter embrace us warmly. When curtains are drawn closed, they keep out draughts and create an introverted environment of safety and security. These translucent fabrics offer exactly opposite charms – they are incorporeal, they veil rather than blocking out light and views. They are not equipped to preserve heat, so are ideal in warm climates or in a heated home with double or triple glazing. Even in a relatively draughty older building, heavier curtains need be hung only during the cooler months. For the rest of the year, let the simple charms of translucent fabrics be the focus at your windows.

There is a wide choice of translucent fabrics available to us, simple or traditional, contemporary or sophisticated – from antique lace panels to the latest sheers perforated by neat rows of holes or seemingly random jagged shapes; from prettily spotted voiles to widely spaced glittery nets in which there is more fresh air than

fibre. Translucent fabric can be roughly grouped into three types: sheers, nets and lace. Sheers include such fabrics as voile (soft, very fine and fluid), organdie (stiffer, traditionally used for frills) and even very thin taffetas (crisp and angular). Nets are woven and any pattern can be formed by the grid of their structure. Lace is formed by knotting, twisting and looping threads into patterns that are fancy and often pictorial.

Translucent fabrics have always had a part to play in a layered effect, usually at the window. An under curtain, or 'glass curtain', in a prosperous Victorian interior was the layer nearest the window. This would be suspended from its own narrow pole and hung either straight or in two pieces, one draped to each side and caught back. The edges on display might be enlivened with a light fringe or bobbled braid. Framing the window itself would be elaborate swathes of richly coloured fabrics, further ornamented with braids and tassels, and even a pair of 'dress' curtains which served no practical purpose.

In the contemporary interior, we are equally likely to be interested in layering, but using a different visual language. A rich, opulent effect can be achieved by laying one open net over another, hung flat or gathered, with the airier fabric to the fore so that you can see the denser layer or layers through it. This is especially glamorous if the nets have reflective fibres in them so that they glitter when the light catches them. Laying nets of different densities over each other, especially when one or more has a glittery thread, is a favoured decorative device of interior designer, author and television personality Orianna Fielding Banks. Layering is not necessary to enjoy the quality of these fabrics, however – their glittery fibres make them equally fascinating on their own.

The simplest translucent fabric is plain, fine-woven cotton. Hung flat or lightly gathered, this most traditional of translucents is immediately at one with the contemporary interior. A home with tall windows, be they elegant Georgian or lofty modern rectangles, is the ideal setting for hanging translucent panels. If properly sealed against draughts, windows need nothing more than a single or double layer of gauzy fabric. Hang a double layer over a pole, and you can loop one layer simply to the side in a graceful curve. With windows where the architectural surrounds are handsome or historical, place a narrow pole to support the curtains inside the window rebate, leaving the architecture of the window uncluttered. This was a device recommended by Edith Wharton, the nineteenth-century novelist and co-author of an influential tome, *The Decoration of Houses* (1897). In her view, architectural detail should not be crowded and cluttered but given space to breathe and be seen.

In contrast to the simplicity of sheer cotton, many contemporary translucent fabrics are simply astonishing. Their magic is generated by the inventiveness of designers, both of the fibres and of the fabrics. Some of these fabrics seem hardly to be with us, being simply a whisper of gauze, more of it cut away than left behind. Some use iridescence or metallic threads to create shimmering fabric with a copper or steely bloom that is nonetheless almost completely see-through. A gingham effect is achieved with glossy viscose fibres in stripes of equal width on warp and weft, the ground fabric being totally transparent cellophane. In another fabric, two extra-fine layers of gauze have trailing coloured fibres imprisoned between them or curling teasingly off the surface.

New technology has made many of these contemporary translucents possible. Modern fibres, many of them microfibres (less than a denier thick, which is very, very fine) can be used to create fragile-seeming textiles that are actually strong and hardwearing. Not only can manmade fibres be extruded or spun in such fine gauges, but many also lend themselves to translucents because they are by nature smooth and transparent until

the manufacturing process roughens their surface, introduces colour or blows them with air to puff them up and give them texture.

In other contemporary translucent fabrics it is the weave which gives interest. Weft fibres on an open-weave translucent are disrupted, bunched to one side or allowed to wander in delicate waves in effects that would have been taken for mistakes in a previous age. Now such deviations are carefully designed, controlled on the loom, and celebrated because we love their off-beat humour and the joy of cleverness in their creation (and because they are simply ravishing to look at).

Among the most surprising and pleasing translucent fabrics are those made from traditional, warming fibres like mohair, a loosely twisted yarn woven loosely to create a gossamer fabric as lightweight as a newborn baby's shawl. Flimsy felt is transformed into a translucent by the simple expedient of cutting dots from it in rows like the holes on a pegboard, while another delightful fabric is formed from lightweight felted woollen stripes separated by near-transparent plain-weave.

Other, more traditional translucents have been re-interpreted through colour. Muslins were available to our forebears in a wide variety of patterns and weaves, but they were usually white. Today, high street stores and mail order catalogues sell readymade tab-headed curtains in glowing, jewel-like colours that bring a bold, ethnic vibrancy into our homes. Panels of different-coloured sheers can be hung gathered like traditional curtains, or flat, alongside each other, in order to conceal a window or as a room divider. Production designer Gianni Silvestri used exactly this device on the set of *Stealing Beauty*, Bernardo Bertolucci's 1996 film shot in Tuscany. In the main bedroom of the farmhouse where it was filmed there was no partition or barrier to demarcate the bathroom – bath and lavatory stood in one corner of a cavernous space. Silvestri hung rails of soft, crumpled muslin panels, alternately grey and tomato red, across the full width of the room to allow the characters some privacy in this corner. Any part of a room – for washing, dressing, work or storage – can be screened off in a similar way.

Arranged on two or more wires or slender rails, different-coloured panels of fabric hung flat or almost flat in front of each will create a kaleidoscope of colour. Open the window and let a breeze lift these lightweight panels so that the colours float and ripple. If you can't get the colours you want from a shop, cotton muslin is easy to dye at home. Alternatively, use lengths of the finest sari silk, with or without elaborately decorated borders, for the ultimate luxurious, brightly coloured, translucent curtains.

Of course, muslins and other translucent fabrics can equally well be used elsewhere in the home, not just at windows. Bed drapes made of translucents have a dreamy, feminine quality and because the fabric is lightweight the supporting structure does not have to be sturdy (though it should be safe). If you have a plain bed rather than a four-poster or half-tester, your drapes can hang from a hook or a piece (or pieces) of dowelling or metal piping suspended from the ceiling. Simply make sure that anything you attach to the ceiling is screwed into supporting joists above, and that you don't pierce plumbing or wiring channels.

A filmy cover for a bed, table or cushion can be given a wide, double hem all round or edged with a more substantial fabric like satin or velvet to give it structure. This is then laid over a solid fabric in a contrasting colour, either deeper or paler, depending on the effect you want to achieve. You can even make a loose cover for a chair from a sheer, though the fabric should obviously be strong enough to bear the weight of an adult sitting on it. The purpose of translucent

covers is not to be practical, in the way of linen or cotton loose covers, but to create drama, sophistication, romance. Because they are semi-see-through, they also add another dimension to the form they are covering. Like gauzy bed hangings, they are essentially feminine in nature.

Any scraps of translucent fabric left over can be used to wrap presents, after you have first concealed the contents with a solid-colour plain or patterned paper. Paint the edge of a fraying fabric (or the line beyond which you don't want it to fray) with clear nail polish. Cotton muslin is particularly versatile for making festive decorations because it knots and drapes well, and is inexpensive. On birthdays, at Christmas or at Thanksgiving it can be wrapped around banisters and swagged along the tops of walls in combination with ivy and evergreens, or bunches of flowers or herbs. You can drape it over pictures and windows, and even wrap and knot it around the pot in which the Christmas tree stands. It was this very quality which endeared muslin to decorators in nineteenth-century Napoleonic France, where it was swagged and draped and trimmed as part of elaborate window treatments.

By contrast, a style like Biedermeier relished the lightness and plainness of muslin panels at the windows because the fabric accorded well with the lightness and relative simplicity of the overall look – its elegant, attenuated lines and the blond woods from which its furniture was formed.

The word 'muslin' originally referred to the very fine cotton yarn from which cambrics, dimity, jaconet, muslinette and ginghams were woven, and then by extension to the entire family of these fabrics. Many muslins had names which referred to their specific use – cheesecloth, butter muslin and flag bunting, for example. Early muslin was spun by the craftsmen of Dacca (now in Bangladesh) and woven into cloth so light and fine (one-quarter of the weight of a contemporary muslin) that it was considered fit only for use at the most exalted and royal occasions.

Until the later eighteenth century, muslins were made only on the Indian subcontinent, but the invention by Samuel Compton in 1779 of the mechanical spinning 'mule' made it possible for the British to spin and hence weave it. This inevitably brought down the price and broadened its use in Europe and America. Many muslins were patterned, with stripes, plaids, ribs or small all-over patterns which might be woven or printed. In the urban home, they were used as much to conceal the ugly views to which people looking out on industrial cities were subjected as they were to prevent prying eyes looking inwards through the windows.

Lace was hugely popular in the nineteenth-century interior, especially once machines had been invented that brought it within the budget of a large proportion of the population. Nottingham in the English Midlands was a great centre of machine lace-making, and some survives there today. Now largely out of fashion for decorating, lace is considered too fussy for the twenty-first century, but to a connoisseur of fabrics it is nonetheless fascinating. And there are, after all, no style police to tell you that you cannot enjoy lace if you want to. Perhaps you'd like to hang an antique panel to conceal an unattractive view, or frame a special piece of lace against a coloured background to display on the wall in order to appreciate it as a piece of fine craftsmanship.

The uses for translucent fabrics today are the same as throughout history – to provide modesty and decoration, and where relevant to protect expensive fabrics like silks by filtering the effects of sunlight. In addition, the pared-down aesthetic underlying the world of choice that is contemporary decorating allows us to enjoy the ghostly delights of translucent fabrics for themselves. Inspiration for the form and style of translucent fabrics in the home can be traditional or modern, retro or classical, western or eastern. (We love the effect of Japanese paper screens.) Translucent fabrics have always been around, but never before in such copious variety, and never in a context where their abstract, tenuous qualities are so celebrated as today.

taffeta

metals

silks

a moiré

ics

atin

sheen

Early morning sunlight on rippling waves sends up sparks of light that **dazzle** us on a seaside summer's morning. The cool sheen of polished stainless steel urges us to reach out and stroke its silken surface. A proud column of mirrored glass – the newest stunning architecture – catches our eye amidst a dusty urban sprawl. It is, after all, our nature as human beings to be drawn to **shiny** things. They don't simply please us; they thrill us with their gleam or **glitter** or sparkle; they bring a smile to our faces, and even make us gasp or giggle with delight.

All fabrics reflect light to a greater or lesser extent, which is how the human eye perceives their colour and depth. But **reflective** fabrics bounce back more light into our eyes than matt fabrics such as plain woven linen or cotton. The result is that our eyes perceive their added sheen. Some, including fabrics coated with minuscule particles of crushed **glass**, are iridescent like mother-of-pearl or insect wings; others, such as heavy **silk** satin, have a rich and deeply sensual lustre. Faux metallic leather is used to upholster chairs and sofas in nightclubs and sophisticated interiors; metallic **sheers** and nets bring new meaning to layered window treatments.

To the touch, these reflective fabrics are smooth and supple, or crisp and crunchy. Whether **hung** as flat panels covering windows in a contemporary interior, arranged in great swathes and swags in a historic house, or quilted and **draped** luxuriously across a bed, what we see with our eyes translates into an emotion of sensual delight and we are halfway to being seduced. In an interior, such fabrics used as curtains and upholstery, lampshades and cushions, tablecloths and even bedlinen (depending on their weight and suitability) entice us with their texture and **play on light**. They possess and project, above all other fabrics, that powerful quality – glamour. In the home, glamour is a modern visual concept – an international film-star quality touched with sensuality and success.

A **glamorous** interior is cool and uncluttered either by objects or patterns or bright colours jostling for attention. It is not a look that reaches out, that demands attention – rather it is subtle and a little haughty, making its impact through understated elegance, a few carefully chosen and placed objects, superb materials and finishes, gleam and **gloss** and polish. There is nothing accidental about a glamorous interior – unlike a bohemian one, which looks as if it has been thrown together or grown organically over time. Glamour is a complete look, every element carefully controlled and calculated for effect. The 1930s spawned some of the most breathtakingly glamorous interiors, such as Rose Cumming's bedroom in her New York apartment, luminous with **silver** wallpaper, silvered furniture and tall windows draped in a waterfall of metallic fabric which fell in folds on the floor. Inspired by Surrealism as much as by Hollywood, Cumming liked to juxtapose metallics with **satin** and raw silk. Another famous room of the period was the bathroom designed by Paul Nash for the actress Tilly Losch in 1932, the walls of which were faced with glass panels, some mirrored, some stippled with a purple sheen (the bath and other fittings were black).

In the 1990s an astonishing untouched 1930s Parisian interior by Jean Dunand and his son Bernard, epitomizing glamour, was revealed when the lady who had commissioned it died at the venerable age of 101. Here, Art Deco met Moderne. Lines were clean and **sleek**. The sofa and chairs in the grand salon were covered in silver-grey satin; at each end of the sofa stood a screen of mirrored panels; a **gilded** and lacquered carved wooden relief of galloping zebras filled one wall. The walls themselves were painted pearly grey and the grey carpet was touched with mauve. Across the sofa was draped a huge guanaco throw. Elsewhere in the flat, reflective surfaces were contrasted with fur – blond rabbit covering the bed and sofas in one room, black fur-covered cushions and pouffe in the smoking room. Sadly, days after a photographic record was made

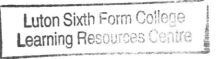

of these fabulous rooms they were dismantled and the contents sold at auction.

The contemporary take on glamour is as pared-down as minimalism, but is distinguished by its use of reflective and contrasting textures, especially in the sumptuous fabrics which give it added depth and sensuality. The bedroom of Vanessa de Lisle, erstwhile fashion editor of British *Vogue*, has pale grey silk taffeta curtains crumpling on to the floor and a darker grey silk duvet cover on the bed laid over crisp white linen sheets. The bedroom created by Site Specific for the London home of an actress is even more glamorous – the padded taffeta curtains and mauve silk quilt contrast with the leather-covered headboard and thick brown fur covering the ottoman, the polished wooden floor and the glittering crystal of a chandelier. In Rome, the apartment of Valentina Buscicchio, whose shop Contemporanea sells the latest furniture designs, is decorated with a mixture of modern and antique pieces. Her authentic 1930s curvy chairs and vast pouffe, upholstered with white satin and deep buttoning, introduce an ice-sharp note of glamour to the interior.

Satin is perennially popular and offers one of the ultimate sensual textures. To feel the slippery smoothness of satin under one's fingers is to experience splendour, even extravagance. Though satins are woven from a variety of manmade fibres including viscose and polyester, and from cotton, the most desirable satin is made from silk. A huge satin-covered quilt draped across a bed transforms it to a scene of self-indulgence or seduction. Satin sheets may be something of a cliché, but they represent the ultimate fantasy in bedlinen. Satin-edged cushions offer a feminine but more serene and contemporary alternative to lace and frills. Dramatic curtains can be fashioned from satin – the heavy fabric hangs fabulously, reflecting both crisp daylight and glowing candlelight with equal hauteur. Small pieces of satin can be used in an interior of almost any style – from colourful bohemian to the most

restrained formality – but it is essentially recognized as a sophisticated fabric.

Satin has its distinctive finish because it is woven with fine silk fibres 'sett' close together on the loom to form the warp of the cloth (the threads that run the length of the fabric). The warp thread is picked up by only about one weft thread in five as it moves across the cloth. This results in threads which seem almost to float across the surface of the cloth. Unlike some other fabrics, where the back and the front have the same look, satin is completely matt on the back, in total contrast to the front. This fabulous fabric has an incomparable glow which lends glamour to the contemporary interior, and catwalk. The artist Winterhalter captured the beauty of satin in the frocks of the nineteenth-century European royalty and beau monde who queued to have their portraits painted by him. Ingres, too, was a master at catching on canvas the way that satin plays with light, its folds embracing shadow while its highlights radiate luminescence. Fashion designers such as Vivienne Westwood and the House of Versace continue to covet the drape and reflective sheen of pure silk satin. This sensual fabric also presents an irresistible visual and textural contrast to so many other desirable furnishing fabrics such as slubby matt linen, rippling velvet and rich damask. It is tempting (and why should we not indulge ourselves?) to introduce a light touch of satin into a room, regardless of its decorative style. Even a minimalist interior will not be unbalanced by a single, pale, satin-covered cushion, and satin easily finds a place in a brocaded drawing room or bohemian boudoir. It is only perhaps in a child's nursery or a rustic kitchen decked with cotton checks and prints that satin might look out of place.

If you plan to work with satin, making your own curtains or covers, bear in mind that it is a fabric which requires some experience. Part of its sensual appeal is its slipperiness. It also tends to fray easily because of the 'floating' threads. Heavy silk satins are expensive, and not practical in the sense that they will show marks and can't be thrown in the washing machine, so it is best to keep them away from children and animals. However, they can be used for upholstery, as well as for cushions and loose covers. Satin doesn't work well as a throw as it is likely to slither off the sofa, but a cashmere or mohair throw can be given a glamorous twist by having a satin border several inches wide around its edge. A cushion cover can have a panel of satin down each side. Satin can also be used to back a cushion made from a fragment of treasured antique fabric, or a small piece of a stunning but fiendishly expensive many-coloured damask cloth.

Reflective fabrics have a long, exalted history. There is no more aristocratic fabric, after all, than lustrous silk, a natural fibre and fabric that has clothed the persons and bedecked the surroundings of the rich and powerful for thousands of years. Some glamorous new fabrics are made by methods which derive from old technology. A reflective finish, for example, can be laid on after the cloth has been woven, by running it through a chemical bath. The cloth can also be burnished on one side after the weaving process is finished, a process akin to the surface being polished, called 'calendering'. This polishing process is the same used to give traditional cotton chintz its shiny finish. A dressing is applied to the front of the fabric and it is then run, face up, between rollers which can be heated. The upper roller is turned faster than the lower one, which creates the friction that brings up the shine, just like polishing a pair of shoes.

Other reflective fabrics are the result of new textile technology. These techno-textiles, invented by chemists, have a dynamic, hip, high-tech profile. In the last years of the twentieth century and the first of the twenty-first, a new generation of fabrics sprang to life, quite different from, though built upon, the technology of earlier manmade fibres such as nylon. The fashion, leisure and sportswear industries have once again taken a lead here, requiring ever more lightweight, high-performance, visually stimulating materials. Concern for the environment is another factor in the creation and manufacture of new fibres. New technology is also being applied to existing synthetic fibres so that, for example, polyester can be permanently pleated or crushed, or have blisters like rows of domes impressed into it (as in Issey Miyake's creations).

Techno-textiles fall into three very simplified groups – synthetics (those largely derived from coal and the petrochemical industry, such as nylon and metallic faux leather), those made from cellulose fibres (for example, viscose, derived from wood pulp) and fabrics made from or including metals. Metals are the easiest to define. They include 100 per cent metal fabric woven from wire or fine threads cut from very thin sheet metal, and supple sheet metal with a design punched into it. Folded or crumpled in the hand, these fabrics stay folded or crushed like aluminium foil. There are also fabrics with only a metal warp or (more usually) weft, and others where metal has been wrapped around another fibre or fibres, so that the metal is only one of several constituents in the cloth. Some fabrics have a metal thread running through them.

While projecting an uncompromisingly modern, even futuristic, look on to an interior, the design influences on some of these metal fabrics are surprisingly earthy. One textile designer, Janet Stoyel, uses the macro lens on her camera to capture images of the cellular structure of mushrooms, which inspire the patterns on her sheet-metal fabrics. Coppery metallic fabric can be as smooth and burnished as an onion skin. Having these metallic fabrics in our homes reflects our excitement at (and enthusiastic acceptance of) developments in new materials and technology, as well as an instinctive delight in glittery things that has not changed since we were children or, historically speaking, since the gilt-tinged days of the Renaissance. We experience the same frisson when we see shiny metal elsewhere, both inside and outside our homes and buildings – from polished copper pans to Frank O. Gehry's latest architectural masterpiece clad in silvery titanium sheeting. To look along the narrow streets of Bilbao, in northern Spain, and see the thrusting curves of his softly gleaming Guggenheim Centre is to experience a lifting of the spirits.

Metallic fabrics can hang loose at windows, or be pulled taut in shutters or panels and screens which divide one space from another in a room. Cushion covers and even bed and table covers can be made from metallic fabrics. But only a substantial fabric with a minor proportion of metal is suitable for seating, either upholstery or loose covers. Metallic fabrics vary hugely in weight and strength, so discuss the possible uses of a fabric with the shop from which you buy it.

Of the three types of techno-textiles, cellulose fibres are those known as 'regenerated' because they are made from nature's own building block, cellulose, which makes up the structure of plants and trees. The first was viscose (also known as rayon). Developed in France and England and patented there in 1892, viscose was first produced by Courtauld's, who bought the patent in 1904. Today, conscious of environmental issues, the company pointedly uses only wood pulp from fast-growing, managed forests that are replanted. Viscose is still popular because of its fine qualities, including lustre, drape, acceptance of dyes and of special finishes, absorbency and hardwearing nature. Designers of textiles for fashion as well as interiors can blend it with other fibres or use it decoratively to give subtle glints to a weave with, for example, linen or wool. A recent development in this family of fibres is lyocell. Spun from vegetable cellulose, it is totally recyclable and biodegradable.

The mother of all synthetic fabrics was nylon, announced by an official of the Du Pont company in America in 1938 as 'a new word and a new material'.

It takes a leap of imagination for us to understand the excitement caused by the fabric and its implications, then and in the following decades. *The Queen* magazine of 13 April 1960 included (alongside 'Mothers and Daughters photographed by Cecil Beaton') an advertisement for nylon sheets: 'Bedmaking is so easy you can do it blindfold... Yes! These sheets wash and drip-dry in a morning! And they're back on the bed, without ironing, before you've even begun to think about lunch. All this, plus the sheer, irreplaceable luxury of smooth BRI-NYLON... textured nylon that will never shrink or stretch, will always keep its good looks, its loveliness, its colour through wash after wash.'

Nylon went out of fashion because it felt hot, held static electricity and didn't quite live up to the manufacturers' promises of remaining lovely with age. The latest synthetic fabrics are more advanced by generations – they breathe, wash beautifully and hold colour, and some are recyclable. Most recent developments in synthetic fabrics include engineered textiles such as non-wovens. Traditionally, fabrics are formed from yarn by the process of weaving or knitting; non-wovens are effectively blown into existence by machinery, forming a web-like surface of randomly laid fibres like the webbing used in dressmaking to interline facings. These 'engineered' fibres can fulfil special functions – one fabric being developed in the USA incorporates fibres which allow air to pass through while filtering out toxins. Created with military uniforms in mind, such fabrics are only a step away from finding their way into the home as window dressing – curtains and blinds of all descriptions – which will purify the fresh air in our homes, especially desirable, of course, in cities.

Microfibres are another promising new area of textile technology. The thickness of a fibre is measured in deniers, one denier being a thread that is 9,000 metres long but weighs only one gram (in other words, almost unimaginably fine). Microfibres are one denier or less and can be used on their own (when they make supremely lightweight, easy-care, hardwearing fabrics used largely in sportswear), or in combination with other fibres to improve their drape and **performance**. Again, we can look forward to them finding their way in due course into the home. Perhaps the most electrifying aspect of this is the way that these fabrics can act as carriers for added ingredients which are slowly released. **Scent** can be added to bedlinen and clothing in this way, as can beneficial vitamins and minerals, and anti-bacterial and other agents. This may have huge ramifications in the textile industry, for both clothing and interiors. It is possible to imagine sheets that help you sleep soundly, for example, and cushions that soothe and **relax** you as you lean back against them.

The **trend** in fabric in the past century has been for the fashion and clothing industry to lead the way in design and technology. Non-woven fabrics and enhanced microfibres are not generally available to us to use on walls and furniture, beds and tables, curtains and covers, but they will be one day. In the meantime our imaginations can anticipate their possible functions, both practical and decorative. **Lycra** caused a revolution in fashion textiles, but it has not yet fulfilled its potential in interiors. Imagine, for example, a blind that you do not draw down or up but stretch out from almost nothing, attaching the edges to hooks or studs fixed at intervals around your window. The concept of fabrics being created and used exclusively for either fashion or interiors is false. No-one will stop you from going into one of the many shops bursting with fascinating and glamorous fabrics and buying them to use in your home, even though they were originally conceived as textiles for outdoor wear or costume. The only limitation on your use of fabric is **imagination**, and the weight and practical fitness of the fabric itself.

Silk is an established star in the firmament of reflective fabrics for use both in fashion and interiors. There are countless styles of **silk** fabric available today, all with a lesser or greater reflective quality. Like satin, they lend

glamour and gravitas to an interior. Some are rough and slubby, with an appearance almost like linen, and are ideal in rooms which tend to the **minimalist**. Others are sophisticated and **complex**, corded and striped, like some of the Jim Thompson Thai silks. Mantua silk has a plain weave but is wonderfully heavy. These silks are at home in a more elaborate interior with polished or gilded antique furniture and **magnificent** curtain treatments.

Among the most popular silks we can use in our homes today is silk **taffeta**, which is lightweight and smooth. In bedrooms, especially, taffeta's brittle elegance translates well into curtains, bed hangings and bed covers. **Drapes** at the window are medium-full, gathered simply at the top and billowing on to the floor to create dramatic light and shadow in the fabric's folds. Line each curtain with a lightweight but thermally effective duvet if you want to lend the fabric body while providing insulation. Taffeta can also itself be used to line curtains made of more substantial materials. In contemporary decorating, pelmets and elaborate swags are superfluous – these curtains make their impact with the sheer **sensuality** of the fabric and its texture. Popular colours are rich browns and reds, and cool pearly shades of grey, celadon green and dusty pink.

For centuries until the middle of the twentieth century (and beyond, in many historic houses), silk was considered the only appropriate fabric for decorating the reception rooms of a wealthy conventional home, and often the **grander** bedrooms too. The choice of silks available for furnishings and fashion from the seventeenth century was extensive – not only plain and ribbed but also brocaded, watered or moiré (a pattern impressed on the finished fabric), taffetas both plain and figured, and even sarsnet (the crisp, lightweight taffeta useful for window dressing). Drawing rooms in particular displayed silk curtains and **upholstery**, which became fuller and more elaborate in the nineteenth century, following the French example. Silk was even used to cover walls. The silks in these rooms were protected from the damaging effect of light by extra layers of curtain and blinds at the windows, and by loose covers on furniture which could easily be removed for grand occasions.

Every design movement and initiative (and many historical events) in the nineteenth and early twentieth centuries in America and Europe embraced silk in one way or another – the Gothic Revival of the 1840s, the advent of 'couture' with Frederic Worth in 1858, the Japanese craze of the 1860s, the opening of Liberty in Regent Street, the Arts and Crafts and Mission Movements, Candace Wheeler, Tiffany, Charles Rennie Mackintosh, the Wiener Werkstätte Studio, Gustav Klimt, Bakst and the Ballet Russe. During World War II Maison Ducharné in Lyons hid its silks from the Nazis while secretly weaving a subversive tapestry. Maps printed on finest silk were easily concealed by resistance workers and spies, and parachute silk was coveted in occupied France (though it could get you into trouble – underwear of certain colours could implicate you in having harboured an Allied airman).

Mariano Fortuny y Madrazo is another important character in a brief review of the power of silk over the years. This Spanish sculptor, painter, photographer, inventor, and stage and dress designer, who died in 1949, is famous above all for his silks. His tightly pleated fabrics were formed into exquisitely romantic evening gowns (surely the forerunner to Issey Miyake's pleats). Silk velvet wallhangings were printed with stylized designs inspired by Renaissance silks, and perhaps by the fabulous embossed leather wallcoverings found in his native Spain. Fortuny silks can still be seen in Venice, where he and his fabrics have come to be identified with and where he restored the fifteenth-century Palazzo Pesaro degli Orfei, making it his home and, initially, his workshop. Taking inspiration from Fortuny's palazzo (now the Museo Fortuny), a relatively small quantity of similar silken fabric (printed or woven

in rich jewel colours) could be used to powerful effect swathed in a single dramatic curtain across an asymmetrical window or hung flat as a panel on the wall in a room furnished with large, dark, carved wooden furniture and lit by soft lamps or candlelight.

Silk has retained its aura of luxury and exclusivity across the centuries, partly because it is still a fabric to be treated with respect, the opposite of a tough, hardwearing utility fabric. Strong when manufactured but vulnerable over time to damp, excessive dryness, light and dirt (its fibres fray from friction with dust and grit), silk takes dye well but its colour can look different from different angles and in different lights. Decorators recommend looking at a length in daylight and by artificial light before making a major investment.

The history of silk is laden with myth and legend, starting with the story of its discovery. Hsi-Ling, the principal consort to the Emperor Huang-Ti of China around 4,500 years ago, is said to have been drinking tea under a mulberry bush when a cocoon fell into her cup. As she fished it out it began to unravel, the hot liquid having dissolved the gluey substance that held it together. She subsequently devoted herself to rearing silkworms and teaching others to do so, and she invented a silk-weaving loom. For two thousand years or more, the cultivation and manufacture of silk was confined to China. It was a symbol of power and favour, its beauty and fame making it a much-sought trading item along what became known as the 'Silk Road'.

India is believed to have acquired Chinese silk-reeling techniques sometime before AD 400. Textured tussah silk, made from the thread of a moth indigenous to India, is still highly prized today. In all countries, silk was valuable and treasured and, as its manufacture spread, countries and cultures admired and absorbed details of each other's design elements. By the dawn of the European Renaissance in the fourteenth century, there was trouble in some silk-producing regions like Persia

(Mongol invaders) and Byzantium (ravaged by the Crusades), but silk was successfully being made in Italy, particularly in Lucca. Here the speciality was repeat patterns incorporating birds and animals, often woven with gold and silver threads, their richness reinforcing our image of Renaissance interiors hung with sumptuous silk brocades and velvets.

In what is now France, in 1309 the Pope moved his court to Avignon, which became established as a famous centre for silk weaving, encouraged by the demand for vestments from the papal entourage. A charming story associated with the French silk industry is that the women carried silkworm eggs around with them in small pouches hung between their breasts, body temperature being perfect for incubating the eggs before hatching. A plague in the early eighteenth century effectively brought an end to this era of thriving silk production in Avignon. The best-known and most successful centre for the manufacture and trading of silks in Europe was Lyons, still famous today. Louis XI gave the town a letters patent in 1466, and in 1531 François I (who required vast quantities of silks for furnishing his luxurious new palace of Fontainebleau) gave the city the status of 'bonded warehouse' for all imported silks which henceforth had to pass through Lyons customs. Lyons maintained its position through the centuries, even in the face the mechanization of the nineteenth century, when it was the quality of its designs that continued to give it prominence.

In seventeenth-century Britain, King James I enthusiastically promoted sericulture. Mulberry trees planted in this period, and their descendants, are still to be seen in the gardens of London's Buckingham Palace, in Stratford-upon-Avon and elsewhere. The silk industry, among other crafts and trades, provided employment for the significant influx into Britain of Protestant Huguenot refugees fleeing religious persecution in the Low Countries and France. Among the craftsmen and industrialists who found refuge and work in England

were the Courtaulds, who arrived in the 1680s. The name is inextricably linked with textile history because it was Samuel Courtauld's company which began production of rayon in 1910 and is still today a textile manufacturer, though ownership of the firm has passed out of the family.

In 1609 James I imported silk-moth eggs into North America through Virginia. For nearly two hundred years there was some form of silk industry somewhere in the colonies – notably Georgia, from where about a ton of silk was exported to England in 1767, and where the trustees of the settlement of Savannah incorporated the silkworm, a cocoon and a mulberry leaf into their official seal. The War of Independence in 1776 dealt the final blow to a crop which, essentially, did not thrive in the climatic conditions and which had already given way to tobacco in Virginia and to indigo and rice in South Carolina.

Silk continued to be produced elsewhere and has never lost its pre-eminent position. Meanwhile, a dazzlingly varied range of reflective fabrics are more widely available than ever before. The finest-quality metallics and other light-reflecting fabrics are still as expensive and exclusive as silk was centuries ago, but the ever-increasing choice of reflectives in the shops today means there is a glossy cloth for every budget. For every sophisticated, sensual or glamorous interior, be the style film-star fantasy or gracious town house, historical period or uncompromisingly contemporary, there is a reflective fabric ready to introduce a note of gleaming sensuality and delight.

patchwork traditional antique idea betty quilting art

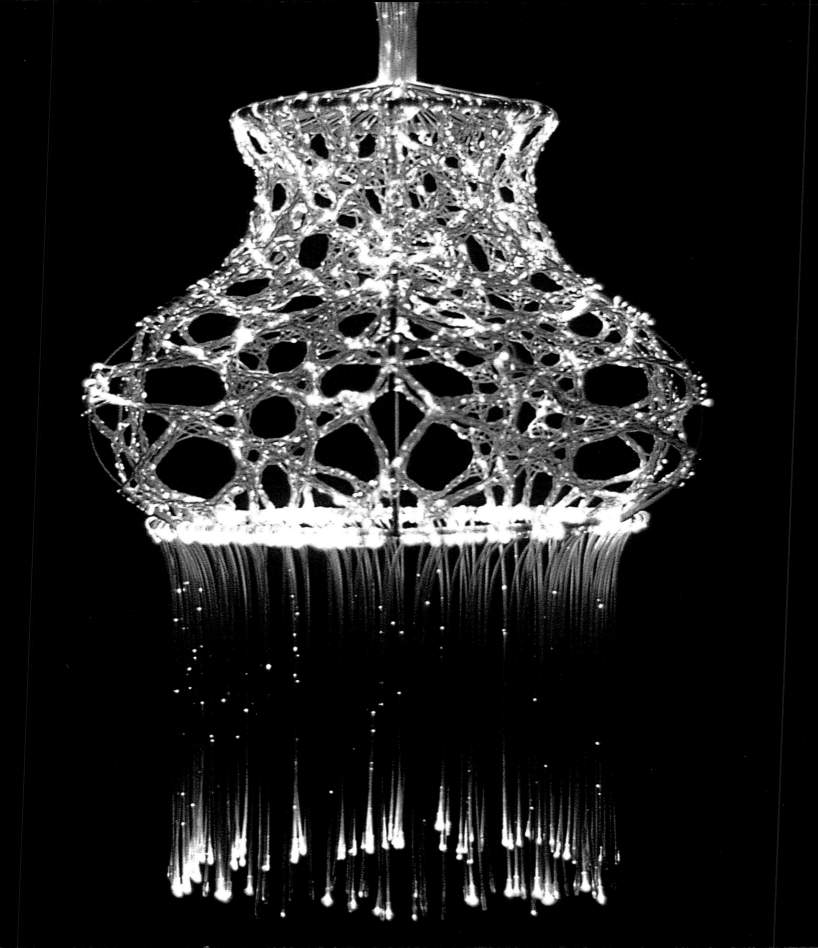

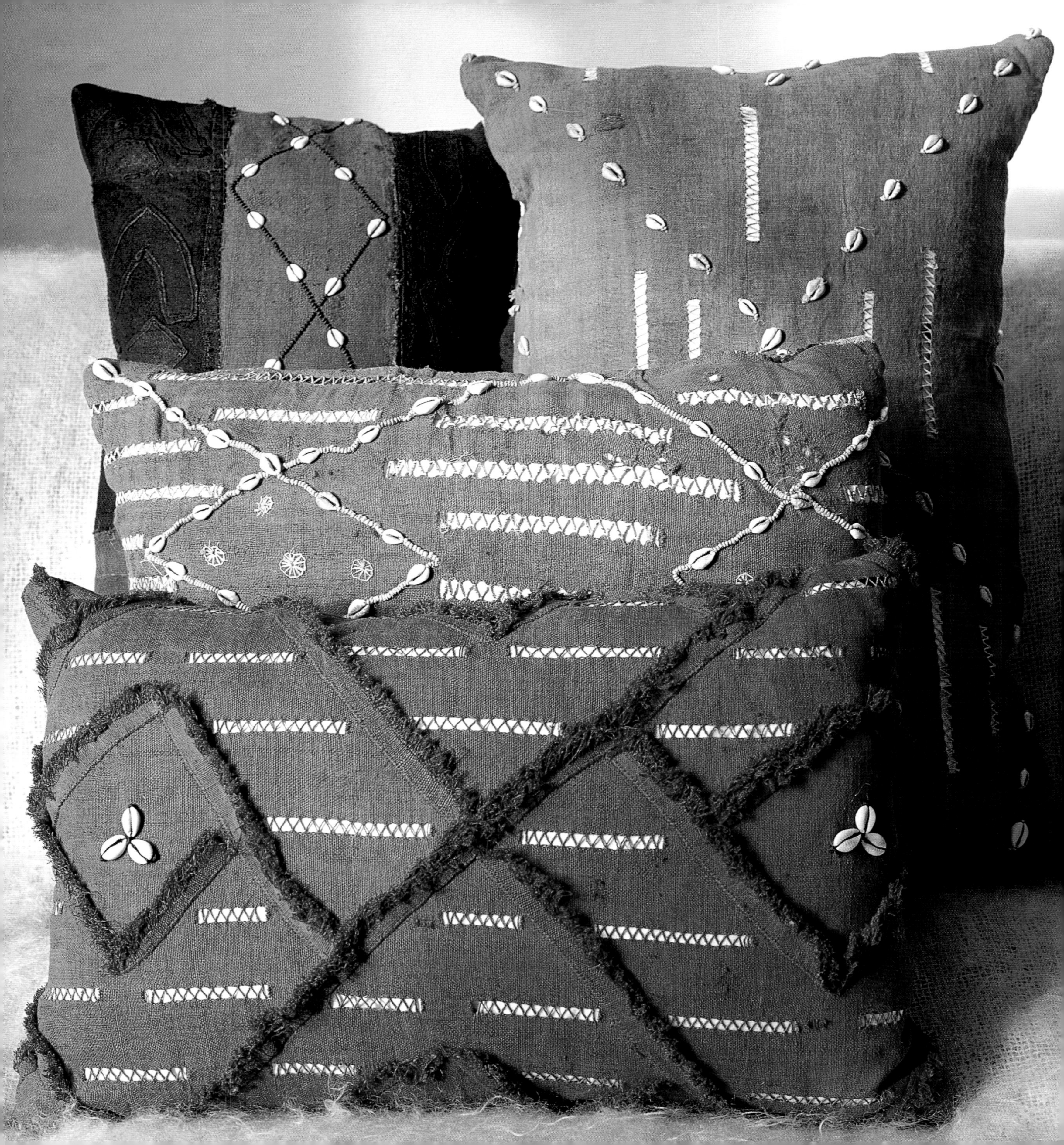

'The effect of su
textured surfac
more interesting
smooth one, and
wheels around a
so the shadows
texture bring a

nlight on a
e is infinitely
than on a
as the sun
uring the day,
it creates on
surface to life.'

Kevin McCloud

Of all the world's rich supply of fabrics, those that are embellished with beads and shells, embroidery stitches and pieces of cloth are the most tactile. Their craggy, knobbly, tufty, overlaid, fragmented or simply uneven surfaces make us want to touch them, to run our fingers over their pronounced textures and feel their roughness and variety. Such textures have the same visual appeal as the skin of an exotic pineapple or the rugged form of a pine cone. Whether beaded or embroidered, fringed, tasselled or appliquéd, these are fabrics to whose rich and complex surfaces our eyes are naturally attracted. In the rooms of our homes they are distinctive, distinguished by their pronounced textures and because their appearance is so detailed and elaborate.

There is a huge abundance and variety of embellished textiles – as many or more types and styles as there are different cultures. This is a precious hoard – encrustations of natural found objects such as pebbles and feathers; incorporation of everyday objects like buttons; vibrantly colourful (or demurely pure white) embroideries spilling out like the emeralds and doubloons overflowing the treasure chests in pirate stories. Embellished fabrics are indeed to be treasured and celebrated. Their richness of texture makes them too special for everyday rough-and-tumble – in spite of our desire to touch and feel their texture, these are textiles to be handled with reverence and great care. Nonetheless, there is a place for embellished fabric in every interior except perhaps the strictly minimalist. Whether the theme of your interior is bohemian or oriental, country house or modern rustic, sophisticated or shabby chic, you can introduce embellishments which will catch the attention and give you pleasure every time you enter the room, at the same time contributing to the real and visual texture of the overall decoration.

Embellished textiles are often a significant ingredient in a fusion or eclectic interior, introducing a note of handcrafted authenticity. A fusion or eclectic interior is one where a wide range of cultural and visual elements are drawn from east and west and often also from different periods, creating an exotic and visually stimulating mélange. The home of designer and retailer Louisa Maybury is just such a space, filled with items from across the world, each a thing of beauty in itself. One corner of the sitting room alone has a worn old leather armchair with cowboy character print cushion, wooden figures from the Philippines, an elegant gilded French chair and gilt Italian mirror, and a mahogany rice jug acting as a door stop. But it is in her bedroom that Louisa displays her collection of embellished fabrics. On the bed is a fabulous pink-green-blue-white quilt from Jaipur, and highly decorated red, green and gold silk saris drape like curtains from a narrow metal rod where they conceal Louisa's clothes hanging behind on rails. A full-length Chinese-inspired scarlet wool coat hangs on the wall like a work of art, one sleeve dramatically embroidered with a huge gold butterfly. In any home, embroidered and embellished garments, shoes and evening bags can become a source of pleasure and visual interest displayed in this way rather than being shut away, stored in cupboards or boxes.

It is possible to trace some themes that run through the great variety of embellished textiles worldwide. For a start, most but not all the embellishments have been applied to the surface of the fabric by hand. This gives them an added individuality, a message about honest labour and pride in work done well, the skills expressed in a thing of beauty created with the human hand, and the power of imagination – a message that flies across the globe from the person who decorated the fabric to you in your home.

Another theme of embellished fabrics is that, in most cases, the decoration and texture have been applied to the flat surface of an existing cloth, as in embroidery and beading. The base material and the materials used to decorate it are equally important – there is no point labouring to ornament a fabric that is either not sufficiently substantial to carry the extra weight, or which is of poor quality and will deteriorate sooner rather than later. The cloth can be made of any fibre – a heavy, slubby linen, a matt, manmade fibre that approximates to this, or the lightest floaty muslin or pure silk. Balance and scale are the keys – decoration on an insubstantial fabric can be visually fine or bold, but it must be light-as-air in weight so that it does not cause distortion or damage. On a substantial fabric, small-scale decoration may be lost or look silly. This is an aspect of ornamentation to remember when choosing your own embellishments in the form of braids or fringes for furniture and curtains.

Not all embellishments are applied by hand, however, and not all have ornament added to a finished fabric that stands alone. On some embellished textiles, the very substance of the cloth creates the decoration. These may be made by machine, as is the case with the wonderful variety of trimmings and tassels available to us, and the fabulous borders on fine silk saris. The entire finished fabric may also be made by hand – brightly patterned felted throws, cushions and hangings created by artists and craftspeople, for example, or origami textiles, or those stalwarts of folk art which have become as modern an artform as they were historical, namely appliqué, patchwork and quilting.

Craftworks such as these originally provided a thrifty method of using up scraps of fabric, or giving valuable imported textiles an extended life. If you are clever with a needle, you can employ all or any of these techniques in the modern context, creating designs that are contemporary both in sweeping style and in specific reference to today's events and concerns, just as patriotic flags and eagles appear on quilts made during America's Civil War. The difference today is that you have a much greater choice of fabrics from which to craft your textile. Patchwork and appliqué can be

used to create a visual link between one area of a room and another. For example, you can apply squares of the fabric you have used as upholstery, loose covers, cushions or a tablecloth on to a blind or curtain at the window, or vice versa. Curtains can be made from different fabrics cut into large squares and sewn together in a chequerboard design. You can also alternate horizontal or vertical panels of a striped or patterned fabric, or pieces of plain bold colour cut from lengths of fabric (or simply using identical tones) used elsewhere in the room's decoration.

High-quality embellished fabrics use techniques such as embroidery which carry the resonance of generations of tradition and history. This is perhaps enhanced when the time or culture from which they come is not our own. We are reminded of gilded medieval paintings, Buddhist temples where statues stand encrusted with coloured glass and mirror, and Russian icons. We may think and wonder about the life of the person who created the object, or we may simply display it with care and pride. Our natural desire to acquire these objects of cultural significance needs to be kept in check, however. Too many different styles of embellished fabric juxtaposed in the same room can become confusing. Instead, choose designs on a particular theme – all eastern, for example, or all with the same colour predominating, or all glittery.

Many embellished fabrics available to us have the added patina of actual age. The nineteenth century produced countless examples of embroidery, whitework and other needlework such as samplers, Berlin woolwork and beading. Ladies in families with any pretension to gentility were often deprived of more than an elementary education (of which needlework was a cornerstone accomplishment) and were forbidden to earn a living. Needlework filled their empty hours as effectively as it did Christmas stockings and charity baskets. It also offered a living of sorts to women of lower class. Many of their embroidered sheets and pillowcases, traycloths and tablecloths have survived as heirlooms or found their way into thrift, antique and interiors shops, and thence into the homes of a new generation who will enjoy and treasure them.

Crewelwork is a richly textured form of embroidery made today in India and sold in department and fabric stores across the world. It usually has gently undulating designs of branches and foliage, birds and butterflies embroidered on to it. Traditionally, these are chain-stitched in white on white (or a creamy shade on cloth of the same colour), in a restrained range of greens and blues, or in a wider variety of colours based on age-old vegetable dyes but including some brighter yellows and reds. Self-coloured crewelwork has a subtle texture that is perhaps more sensual, while the coloured yarns add greater visual texture to a room. Both types make handsome hangings and bed covers, and accessories such as cushions, but neither is ideally suited to use as upholstery because their decoration is essentially fragile and will not withstand wear. Though crewel fabric makes fine, billowing, closely gathered curtains, to enjoy the embroidery to the full it should be only lightly gathered or almost flat. Alternatively, hang it in panels which are gathered only in a few points at intervals across the top. At each of these points attach a loop, from which the panel can be hung from hooks on the wall or from a pole across the top of a window or door.

The pioneer women of North America – in a manner similar to ladies in the drawing rooms of England and New York – turned to needlework for enjoyment and occupation when they could get the materials. Crewelwork was popular, embroidering pictures and patterns in two-ply, loosely twisted woollen yarn on to (usually) plain, often undyed cotton or linen, using a variety of stitches. American needlewomen adapted their stitches to use as much yarn length as possible on the front of the cloth, with as little as possible of this precious commodity hidden on the back. They

chose their subjects from the animals and birds, trees, flowers and objects around them, with charming results.

Antique textiles such as these have a distinct appeal. Their mellow colours and often the physical evidence they carry of age and a past life contribute to a sense of history which they bring with them into your home. Pieces of antique fabric, including tapestries, can be found in antique shops and also in less exalted (and often less expensive) settings like antique fairs, auctions and even flea markets. You may be able to track down an antique chair or stool upholstered with its original fabric. If you own any antique textile, you will want to display it to best advantage while ensuring that it is safely preserved for future generations to enjoy. For information about the care of antique fabrics, see Chapter Eight, Fabric for Real.

As well as texture, colour is always a significant element on embellished fabrics, and so frequently is reflectivity. Shaped fragments of mirror enliven the surfaces of some embroidered Indian fabrics, frequently seen in the west on dresses, handbags and cushions. Beading has never been more popular, understandably so since the little sparkling coloured glass pieces create a sort of magic on the surface of the fabric, adding not simply texture but life. The twinkle of light refracting off the beads creates a sense of movement. Beading has a crystalline appeal akin to sugar crystals – it looks almost good enough to eat.

On some embellished fabrics the decoration covers the whole surface, while on others it provide accents. Trimmings, known as passementerie, give a finish and flourish to curtains, upholstery, cushions and other furnishings. The choice of trimmings today includes many which would have been familiar to a Victorian upholsterer, such as the heavily fringed bullion which adds visual and physical weight to the bottom of loose covers, tablecloths and the edge of substantial curtains and pelmets. Gimp is an openwork braid, widely used by upholsterers for covering pins around the edges of furniture. Other trimmings are uncompromisingly contemporary, for example, those incorporating feathers or seashells, or paper or grass ornaments. Always bear scale in mind when choosing trimmings like these – the effect of an exquisite, delicate or detailed braid may be lost on a large piece of furniture, while a heavy, bold trimming may overwhelm a small item. Passementerie has been used on its own to cover an astonishing chair by V.V. Rouleaux of London. On every inch of its upholstered surface have been stitched lengths of tactile and colourful braiding, pompoms, fringing and beads – a humorous tribute, if one were needed, to the often overlooked visual and textural impact of trimmings.

Some embellishment is purely abstract, decoration for its own sake, which may also have the effect of drawing our attention to the material which provides the embellishment. This is the case with a cushion sewn with squares of mother-of-pearl in rhythmic, regimented rows. While figurative decoration is usually stitched, abstract designs often use purely functional stitches to secure decorative items to the cloth. The design of some embellished fabrics incorporates both decorative stitching and applied decoration. In Thai appliqué, borders constructed from strips of brightly coloured cloth are punctuated by bands of stitching in other, contrasting colours, and the body of the textile has repeating geometric shapes formed from appliquéd folded cloth interspersed with embroidery. Cushions or chair backs covered with bold, colourful textiles like Thai appliqué fit well into any interior that is similarly bold and colourful – be it spacious modern rustic, where such a piece will be a focus of attention, or crowded ethnic or bohemian, where it will join many other hand-crafted pieces bursting with character.

Other decoration on embellished fabrics is pictorial, showing representations of people, animals, plants, flowers, birds, insects and places that we (or certainly their creators) can recognize. Sometimes the images have a symbolic or religious significance – the Virgin of Guadalupe, patron saint of Mexico, on embroidery from Coahuila and Puebla, for example, or devils and angels dancing around the sun on a wallhanging from Hidalgo, also in Mexico. The home of make-up artist Charlie Green in New York displays an eye-popping mixture of embellished textiles celebrating the religious and the royal – an embroidered and painted wallhanging of Our Lady of Fatima alongside Union Jacks and portraits of the Queen. A note of irony is introduced by the Jamie Reid print 'God Save the Queen: Sex Pistols' hung on the wall (the words like torn-out newsprint, plastered across Her Majesty's face), and the whole effect is relieved by shaggy animal-print cushions and throws, large flower prints and a vintage embroidered cushion of the Stars and Stripes on the daybed.

Pictorial decoration on embellished textiles is usually stitched, and has a particularly direct appeal to us as it tells us something about the environment from which the object has travelled. With items made specifically for export, however, it is always possible that the designs have been created with the market where they will be sold in mind. If so, the embroidery continues a long tradition of design influenced by the taste of possible buyers, of which Indian palampores offer a venerable example. These bed hangings, which were decorated with flora, fauna and sometimes huntsmen or the Tree of Life, were created in seventeenth- and eighteenth-century India for the European market, and started a craze for floral fabrics which eventually led to the huge popularity of printed chintz. The pictures were often the makers' puzzled interpretation of designs supplied to them by agents of the British East India Company, who believed they would satisfy European demand. This does not make such textiles less 'authentic', it is a charming example of design influences which can be traced across the world and through history.

Today, too, the significance of market forces, the global market and the ways in which demand for embellished fabrics is directed and stimulated by retailers in the developed countries cannot be over-estimated. It is not just by happy coincidence that a resurgence of interest in embellished fabrics is matched by their wide availability in our shops at prices to suit every budget. Partly this is inspired by the fashion industry. Beading and embroidery have been among the great skills of craftspeople in the couture industry for centuries. Under leading couturiers like Christian Lacroix and Vivienne Westwood these skills have seen something of a renaissance, and the trend has filtered down through the market. Our familiarity with flamboyant folk costume has also contributed to the welcome we have given embellished fabrics – images of gypsies and London's pearly kings and queens, not to mention the exoticism of national costume in Asia and the Orient, have become accessible to us through magazines and television, and increased ease of travel.

An item may not necessarily have been made in one place only. If a designer wants to achieve a particular effect, he or she can source embroidered fabric in India, import shells or pieces of mother-of-pearl from, say, the Philippines, and have them applied to the embroidered fabric in the destination country. This is exactly how Steve and Louisa Maybury make their fabulous bed coverings. Rare and exclusive, these are made for interior designers by commission only because of the high cost of the finished textile.

Stylists and trend predictors have a significant part to play too. These are the behind-the-scenes gurus of the fashion and interiors industries whose predictions of shifts in taste and style, from broad movements to details of colour and finish, are avidly followed by the retail industry and command exorbitant fees. Their predictions strongly influence the fabric and other furnishing and decorating items we find in our shops. Even the flower industry has its own analysts, who advise their subscribers on which blooms will be in demand in a few seasons' time. It can take years for the results of these predictions to arrive in the shops, however, because of the time it takes to source and manufacture every element, from the right-coloured thread to details of the finish. At the climax of the process, exquisite little bags and hats and beaded bracelets are to be found in the world's fashion accessory departments and shops, as are similarly decorated cushions, mats, lampshades and other accessories in our interiors stores.

Embellished fabrics and fabric objects bring an element of charm and craftsmanship to the rooms of our homes. Each piece is individual, and our choice of that piece reflects in turn our own individuality. An appliquéd or embroidered cushion is thrown on the sofa with others which offset its particular colours and detailing; an antique patchwork quilt is spread welcomingly across a bed; a pretty beaded fringe glitters and trembles on the lower edge of a lampshade – such embellishments add both physical and visual texture, in the most delightful ways imaginable.

toile d

abstract & re

toile d

artis

provençals

Printing puts pattern on fabric. It also brings texture of a different sort into our homes – not the type you can touch, but **visual texture**. Imagine a room with no pattern, then in your mind introduce cushion covers, curtains or a piece of furniture upholstered in a **striped** or checked pattern or an abstract or **floral** print. See at once how this alters and enriches the composition of the room. The reason is that **pattern** introduces visual complexity; it teases and tickles our eyes pleasingly. It adds interest.

Pattern can be huge and dramatic in a room with scale to match, or small and delicate. It can be subtle, in shades of white and neutral or other closely related tones in a subdued interior scheme, or bright and vibrant in a post-modernist or bohemian context, its colours joyfully **jostling** like the oranges and lemons in a fruit bowl. Everywhere we look in the world around us there are patterns – some regimented like rows of tulips in a Dutch market garden, or garments on a rail in an exquisitely sophisticated city store; some seemingly chaotic like leaves on the branches of a tree, or random like sand dunes in the desert. Regimented or random, pattern is always **stimulating** to the eye.

You can use as little or as much pattern in your home as pleases you. After all, contemporary decorating is all about choice. Occasionally a home appears in the magazines that is a riot of colour and pattern, brilliant shades (sometimes several) in every room, shapes and patterns jostling each other over painted, printed, woven surfaces in a heaving mass of **visual energy**. Quite often this is the home of an artist or designer, because people whose professional business is concerned with the way things look have the confidence to be visually outrageous. Also, perhaps, they have a heightened visual **sophistication** which enables them to enjoy a complex scenario.

Gianni Versace's house in South Beach, Miami, springs to mind as an example, but he was by no means the only designer whose home is a cornucopia of pattern. The astonishing interior of Sue Timney's farmhouse on a Scottish island is a mixture of boldly patterned **African**, Mexican and Swedish textiles and artefacts, children's art and tartan, all set against a backdrop of Scottish pine floorboards and cladding and views of the Mull of Kintyre. This multi-cultural jumble of patterns is highly personal (Sue Timney is of Scottish extraction but was born in North Africa) and, while equally strong, is in stunning contrast to Timney Fowler's cool, sophisticated fabric designs drawn from **classical** Greek and Roman art and architecture. Such interiors as these induce in most of us astonishment and a kind of mental indigestion. We find them overwhelming, although we enjoy the **spectacle** and may well pick up some ideas to adapt to our own needs and desires.

Everywhere in the **bohemian** interior of an artistic person such as Sue Timney there are colourful, personal objects and decorating quirks that reflect the owner's creativity, and that of his or her family and friends. There is a certain amount of **clutter** – books, pictures, objects, hats, strings of beads, bowls of shells or stones, and other mementoes of a varied and creative life. There is colour and pattern. By its very nature, bohemian style is organic, built up over time rather than put together by a decorator. It may be quite smart or reassuringly shabby, but it is always welcoming, drawing you in with its warm humanity.

How much pattern you want in your rooms is essentially a matter of personal **taste**. A few exquisite cushions might be all you need to make you comfortable, or you may be a person who likes large-scale curtains covering your windows... or something in between. You may enjoy plenty of pattern in one room – for example, a cheerful rustic kitchen with **provençal** or retro patterned tablecloths and napkins, and children's art on the walls – while another room is dominated by smooth surfaces of flat colour and texture. If you are not sure how much pattern to have, start small and get bigger.

Keep a scrapbook or reference board of fabric samples and pictures of interiors you like. Consider changing with the seasons – simple floaty sheers at your windows in summer, replaced with warming, patterned curtains in winter to distract from the dreary weather and leafless trees outside.

This eclectic, flexible approach is a million miles from the conventional attitude to patterned fabric in decorating. Traditionally, the advice was to select your primary pattern first when decorating a room, then to draw colours from it and find other patterns to complement it. This is a perfectly valid approach, and a good one if you are planning on large, elaborate window treatments in keeping with a period interior, or curtains made in a particularly expensive fabric. The cost of these dictates that the patterned fabric elements will be an important, possibly the most important, feature of the room. But with the change of emphasis to integrity of surfaces, simplicity and unfussiness that the new millennium has brought with it comes also an attitude to decorating that allows you freedom to break 'rules'.

The world of patterned fabric has several stalwarts. These include crisp, straight-line patterns which are frequently woven into the cloth, like stripes, checks and tartan. Other stalwarts are printed designs such as toiles de Jouy, provençals, and flower patterns on chintz and other natural fibres. In the last hundred years, new genres have proved popular and lasting – character prints, artists' prints, abstract designs, camouflage. Toile de Jouy, or simply 'toile', is one of the most famous styles of printed patterned fabric that has passed the test of time and has, if anything, become increasingly popular in recent decades. The term 'toile' is derived from one particular fabric made in the eighteenth century at Jouy-en-Josas in France, namely monochrome scenic designs. Because these consist of two colours (the background cloth and the printed colour), toile is easy to mix with other patterns which have been printed or woven in the same palette for a sophisticated,

many-layered continental look. Checks and stripes are fresh and give a contrast to the sinuous lines and detail on toile. Small, all-over prints often go well with it, as do plain fabrics with flat colour in a related tone, such as velvet or a slubby linen. Toiles can be used in any way that fabric is used to decorate rooms, from large-scale curtains or wallcoverings, stretched between battens screwed to the plaster, to details like cushions or table napkins. The mood they create is historic but not fussy or frilly.

Many of the ideas for combining toile with other fabrics in our homes apply equally to any patterned fabric. Neutrals go well with toile and have a light and calming effect, preventing the toile from seeming too busy, as does a solid colour used somewhere in the room to provide an anchor. When hanging curtains made from a toile fabric, make the length generous but do not gather the fabric tightly – keep it fairly loose and flat so that the pictures on the pattern can be appreciated.

Though toile is now the name given to any fabric with monochrome scenic designs, this was in fact only a part of the original factory's output at Jouy. The proprietor, Christophe-Philippe Oberkampf, neither invented the toile de Jouy style of patterned fabric nor was the first to print it (Robert Nixon was printing this kind of fabric in Ireland in 1752). Toile de Nantes was also made in Nantes, then part of Brittany, during about the same period as at Jouy. Oberkampf produced many other styles of print that were equally or more successful at the time, especially multicoloured floral designs and *ramoneur* (meaning 'chimney sweep') patterns, so-called because of their dark backgrounds which were usually black, purple or deep plum.

The subjects embraced by toiles provide a romp through history. Hardly a major battle or political event was ignored in the eighteenth and nineteenth centuries. Designs also included historical monuments across the world, mythology, children playing games, the four continents, the arts, the elements, the seasons, sports, seafaring trades and literary characters. Industry was the subject of a famous toile made at Jouy ('Les travaux de la manufacture', 1783–4), alongside more familiar pastoral scenes like 'Les occupations de la ferme' (c.1785–90). There was no limit beyond imagination and decency to the subjects a toile might portray.

The history of the manufacture of printed fabrics encompasses over the centuries hand-carved wooden blocks, engraved copper plates, wooden and copper rollers, flat screen printing and roller screen printing. Toile was made by the engraved copper plate process, with the first printed fabric the Oberkampf factory produced appearing in May 1760. Oberkampf insisted on the highest quality at every stage, from the artistic skills of the designers to the chemicals or 'drugs' used, and the employment of experienced labourers from Switzerland. The cotton on which he printed had to be of good quality (much of it was made in India and bought in London), and dyes had to be colourfast. Anything else was a false economy. It was also important always to be ahead of your competitors. On one occasion, an Oberkampf employee visiting factories in England feared that his notes of technical observations (effectively, industrial espionage) would be confiscated by customs officials. Accordingly he wrote his records in mordant on undyed cloth – invisible to the naked eye – and stacked it among other samples. Once back in Jouy, this cloth was dipped in dye which adhered where the mordant had been painted, and the writing appeared as if by magic.

Figurative pattern – designs incorporating pictures of actual things such as people, trees, scenes, birds, and especially flowers – is a mainstay of printed fabric. English chintz of the later eighteenth and nineteenth centuries is firmly associated in the popular imagination with floral patterns and the country house *style anglais* epitomized by the interiors of John Fowler, Sybil Colefax and Nancy Lancaster (all of Colefax and Fowler) and,

latterly, Nina Campbell. Other influential international decorators and designers who loved such floral fabrics include Dorothy Draper, Geoffrey Bennison and, today, Nicky Haslam. *Le style anglais* survives and thrives in a fresh interpretation for the twenty-first century as seen in the home of interior decorator Polly Fry. Cool, muted colours on walls and floors act as a backdrop to, and calming influence on, a mixture of different floral designs in different colours, not only on fabric but on objects and architectural detail – and of course as a backdrop for great bowls and bunches of real roses and lilies, azaleas and geraniums.

Manufacturers such as Sanderson in the twentieth century made a wide choice of floral fabrics available to the middle-class market. These drew on recent traditions of floral fabrics, including the attenuated plant and floral forms favoured by Art Nouveau designers, C.F.A. Voysey and the Silver Studio (championed by Liberty of Regent Street) and, before them, the master of flower and plant designs, William Morris, whose patterns are still available after more than a century. Today, contemporary decorating allows flowers in simplified, highly stylized forms and in huge photographic close-ups covering whole walls. Classic floral chintz and linen unions, meanwhile, are still to be had from historic textile firms such as G.P. & J. Baker, as well as Colefax and Fowler and Geoffrey Bennison, while Fired Earth produces a cotton and jute fabric whose design is directly related to Moghul flower patterns found on textiles of the late seventeenth or early eighteenth century.

Flowered fabric has proved a perennial favourite, surviving all other fashions in home furnishing and effortlessly crossing generations, centuries, countries and cultures. The Moghul court may have crystallized and disseminated stylized flower designs on fabric in the seventeenth century, but they in turn were inspired by English herbals, precious books brought as gifts by ambassadors from England, and by European tapestries and paintings. Chinese textiles bearing a lotus design and Italian woven velvets and silks are also believed to have influenced the Moghuls. These lines of influence and interpretation of flower images can be traced, and are fascinating in themselves, but shouldn't distract from the simple fact that it is part of the human condition to love flowers, their colour, scent, forms and transience. This love has provoked visual representation which has at certain times in history risen to a fine art that has found expression specifically in fabric designs. Two such periods are notable. The first was during the reigns of the Moghul Shahs in the first half of the seventeenth century, originally inspired by the spring flowers of Kashmir. The second was the years 1825–60, known as the period of 'muscular' textile design in Britain and France. In America at this time the textile industry was striving to make affordable household and clothing fabrics for the general population, so those who wanted and could afford them turned to imports from Europe for something more colourful and flamboyant (and exclusive), usually large-scale, exuberant floral designs.

Another idiom of floral fabric design that transcends fashion is the provençal – brilliantly coloured printed fabric bearing a variety of repeating flower motifs, some more naturalistic, others more stylized. Provençals originated in the enthusiasm for painted and printed Indian fabrics imported into France through the port of Marseilles during the seventeenth century, which were copied and were all the rage at the court of Louis XIV. By the nineteenth century, however, their sun had been eclipsed. Their revival is probably due to the discovery in 1938 by Charles Démery of an astonishing stash of around forty thousand original wooden printing blocks belonging to the fabric-printing company he had acquired. His company, Souleiado, revivified these patterns and promoted them across the world.

In the twentieth century, one of the most interesting phases in the history of printed fabrics was 'artists'

prints'. Established painters and sculptors were used to breathe new life into the design of fabrics. Design has always been recognized by the best industrialists as of primary importance alongside quality and technological performance in the production of fabric. Superior design contributed to the success of Oberkampf's enterprise at Jouy and the survival of the silk industry of Lyons. Modern industrialists consequently worry about the promotion of technical skills over artistic ones in today's textile design training courses. Textile designers in history are so often anonymous. Artists' prints brought the craft into focus, and brought into our homes designs by (to name a few) Raoul Dufy, Duncan Grant, Alexander Calder, Henry Moore, Barbara Hepworth, John Piper, Victor Vasarely, William Scott, Howard Hodgkin, Eduardo Paolozzi and David Hockney, while others worked in a visual idiom recognizably that of Andy Warhol and Roy Lichtenstein. Today the boundaries between textile design and fine art are sometimes blurred, as in the work of Sharon Ting, Neisha Crosland, Sonja Flavin (working with knitted fibre optics), Emily Dubois and the Japanese textile artists. Ting and Crosland are particularly well known in interiors circles, Ting for her colourful hand-printed designs on silks and silk velvet, and Crosland for her classically elegant, curvilinear and repeated designs on fabric accessories such as cushions, and latterly also on wallpaper. Machiko Agano is a leading Japanese textile artist, her delicate constructions made from silk organza and bamboo fanning out like feathers on the wing of a bird.

Artists' prints were just one manifestation of a great upsurge in vibrant design that began in Europe and America in the 1950s. The dreary days of the war were past and people dared once again to be optimistic and to look to a brighter future. Furniture companies like Heal's in London, and Knoll and Herman Miller in the United States, led the way in commissioning new, uninhibited and colourful fabric designs from designers such as Alexander Girard, an architect with an inspiring collection of **folk art**. In Italy, creative names still familiar to us over fifty years later, such as Ettore Sottsass and Piero Fornasetti, became involved in textile design. Scandinavian designers such as Astrid Sampe in Sweden and in Finland the Marimekko team of Armi Ratia, Maija Isola and Vuokko Eskolin-Nurmesniemi were also prominent. In Britain, Lucienne Day was possibly the most prolific of a group of designers of fabric that included Marion Mahler, Terence Conran and Jackeline Groag. Patterns were self-consciously contemporary, loosely **geometric**, employing both lines and shapes, sometimes overlaid. Design influences included the work of artists like Calder, Paul Klee and Jean Miró. Today, interest in these fabrics and their designers has revived, with Habitat (child of the same Terence Conran) selling duvet covers **printed** with an original Lucienne Day design, and a lively market in authentic fabrics, furniture and furnishings from the 1950s and 1960s in shops and salerooms. The best of these pieces fit effortlessly into our homes today, provided they are surrounded by simple modern or contemporary design. In spite of their age, they retain a sense of **modernity** and fun.

Another manifestation of printed fabric design in the twentieth century is the 'conversation print' – light-hearted and sometimes **kitsch** in the sense that it rejoices in a colourful vulgarity. This flaunting of convention can set the tone for an entire interior look, vibrantly colourful, individual and eclectic. Conversation prints have an all-over design and a sense of humour, and their intended destination was not the home's reception rooms but kitchens, bathrooms, dens and children's rooms. From the 1920s, when children's comics first appeared, simply drawn and often **narrative** designs crept on to wallpaper and textiles. An idealized Old West, complete with cactus plants and wagons, sailing boats, the circus, firemen and soldiers, nursery rhymes, children with dogs or dolls, outer space... these were some of the subjects served up with a hearty dose of cheerful optimism and **nostalgia**.

Some forms of textile patterning are so new that we do not yet know how lasting they will prove. Computer-generated designs are printed by ink-jet technology similar to that used in the type of ink-jet printer we may have attached to our **computers**, while soundwave patterning is environmentally friendly in that it uses no chemicals or dyes to produce its effects. Setting aside these technologies untested by time, and the fabrics whose pattern is **woven** into them, most patterned fabric is still machine printed by conventional means. Some ethnic and craft fabrics are printed by hand or patterned by the resist or discharge methods (see Chapter Seven). There is a handful of companies around the world – if that many – where the finest block-printed fabric is executed by hand for a small but significant body of discerning and wealthy customers. Most of the patterned fabric available to us, however, has been printed in factories on machines of increasing power and versatility.

Technology transformed the business of making fabric almost beyond recognition, in the developed nations at least, between the last decades of the twentieth century and the early decades of the twenty-first. **Looms** became almost unbelievably fast and powerful. To some extent this has been a factor in keeping the western textile industry alive (because fast output has made the fabric produced economically viable) in the face of low labour costs in the east. There has been similar progress in the speed (and economic viability) of fabric **printing**, though the best-quality fabric is not printed as fast as products lower down the market.

Fibres also have to be stronger in order to withstand being woven at high speed. Designers often therefore incorporate polyester, or Trevira, into fabrics because it lends strength to other fibres. One of the sources of pride in the American cotton-growing industry is the fact that the strength of their cotton staple is progressively increasing, which makes their product more appealing than others to fabric manufacturers.

An intriguing aspect of fabric design at the beginning of the twenty-first century is the huge popularity of **camouflage** for use not only on fashions but in interiors. How did such a trend begin? Perhaps with young people wearing army surplus, a street-cred element picked up and exploited by couturiers as a witty weapon in the style wars. The ultra-establishment, armed forces connotation seems to have been lost along the way, and camouflage has gained high fashion credentials. Now it can be seen on the **catwalk**, on Dior evening wear and accessories, for example, and in the high street in the form of bikinis, shirts and even footwear. Interior designers have used it to dramatic effect – **graphically** illustrated by the home of Jean-Charles de Castelbajac, where sofas and even antique chairs are upholstered in camouflage. No longer are its colours limited to the greens and browns used by the military – they now include purple, pink or turquoise.

The origins of camouflage fabric designs are entirely serious, however. The word 'camouflage' came into being in 1917, derived from the French *camoufler* which means 'to make up for the stage', but the idea of soldiers' **uniforms** helping them blend into their environment may go back as far as 1795 when members of the New York militia were dressed in green. In the mid-nineteenth century British soldiers in desert regions began to wear khaki and stained their white pith helmets to match, using tea. The first uniform item to be decorated with the variously coloured blotchy design we think of today as camouflage was the *stahlhelm*, a deep-sided helmet worn by German stormtroopers in 1916. During the Second World War, while the British and other armed forces were still dressed in khaki or green or white (as appropriate to the theatre) the American army led the way with a reversible splodgy design know popularly as the 'frog' pattern, created by the gardening editor of *Better Homes and Gardens* magazine, Norvell Gillespie. This proved not to be ideal – among its drawbacks was the fact that the brown colours washed out to a bright shade of pink.

Today there are hundreds of military camouflage designs used by armies across the world, their number swelled by the break-up of the USSR and countries like Yugoslavia – each new state must have its own camouflage as a badge of independence. Technology has increasingly encroached on camouflage. Since the Vietnam War, military designers have incorporated infrared **reflectants** into camouflage.

Newer developments include using low-reflectant dyes to combat night sights, 'ghillie' suits with loose strips of cloth to defeat thermal imaging, and the use of computers to produce equations of a landscape's colour components for reproduction on fabric. Possibly the most exciting development is the incorporation of minuscule light-sensitive chemical sensors which would **change colour** according to the terrain, a prospect that must have designers in the worlds of fashion and interiors beside themselves with feverish anticipation.

This passion for camouflage is only one of the latest manifestations of our love of pattern, not always chosen from the predictable canon of fabric for interiors. There is room for **novelty** and fun in the way we use patterned fabrics in our homes – they are, after all, designed to be stimulating to the eye, the imagination and sometimes our sense of humour.

Fashions change, however, and classic printed patterns inevitably outlive the passing fads. If you don't want to miss out on the fun, use new and exciting patterns in small areas – blinds or curtains for smaller windows, for example, and accessories like cushion covers and lampshades. Then wait to see if their look survives the passage of time. If not, move on to another amusing **pattern**. If they do pass the test, and your love grows too, you can expand your scheme to include larger areas of pattern such as whole window dressings. Patterned fabric will enrich your rooms with visual texture, making them more interesting and effortlessly helping to set the mood and define the style of your home.

red

contrasts & c

ethnic

prints

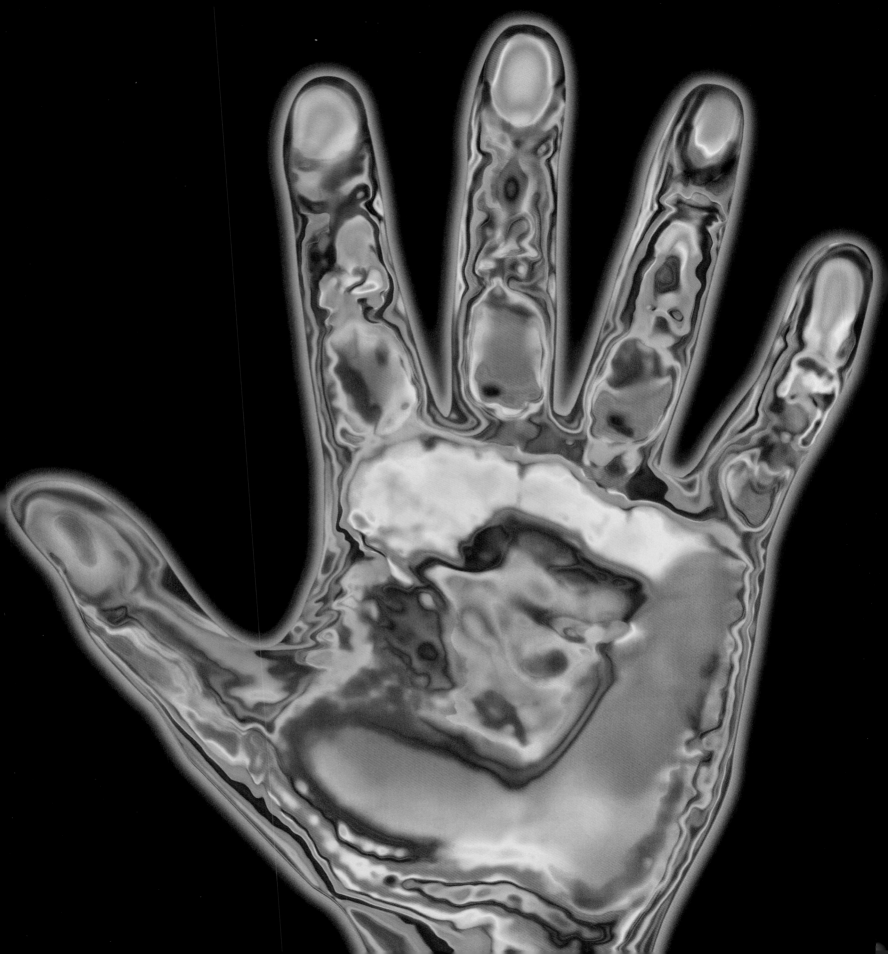

The thrilling emotional and visual power of **colour** is one of the greatest tools at our disposal for decorating our homes in the twenty-first century. Brilliant berry **reds**, blues that remind us of tropical seas and skies, verdant and vibrant **greens**, glowing browns, pellucid greys and neutrals... we can take our pick of these and all the other countless **shades**, tones and textures available to us to colour our walls and floors and furniture, and to dress our windows. For inspiration, we can look at fabrics and interiors, art and artefacts, landscapes and luscious fruits and flora from across the **world**, from the Americas across Europe to the Arab and Muslim worlds, from Scandinavia to Australasia, from Africa to Asia.

There is a veritable **rainbow** of fabrics from which we can choose to enliven our rooms and contribute to their visual texture. As with pattern, so with colour – even the simplest, plainest fabric, if it has distinctive colour, introduces variety and interest into a decorative scheme. Colours set next to each other create a delicious frisson. Plain-woven fabrics can be used to contrast with fabrics of the same colour but more distinctive texture – rougher, hairier, smoother or silkier. This is **visual texture**.

Colour in the home today falls into five general groups: bright colour, deep colour, **muted** colour, pale colour and neutrals. Bright colours include scarlet, orange, turquoise and sunshine yellow. **Deep** colours include the lovely glowing russets, pea greens and grey-blues found in historic colour ranges. Muted colours are softer, less dynamic versions of these – safe, gentle and unimposing shades like sage green and dusty pink. **Pale** colours are those with plenty of white in them. White and **neutrals**, including grey, are useful to offset any of the other groups.

Choosing fabrics whose colours combine well in a room and meld with the colour of other surfaces is a task which is entertaining to some of us, while others find it problematic. Think of choosing fabrics to **decorate** your room in the same terms as putting together an outfit. Decide on a prevalent colour group, then add a background neutral and a colour of **contrasting** weight. This could be a deep colour to act as an anchor if your chosen group is pale or a bright one to act as an accent if your prime colours are deep, just as you would add a scarf, belt, handbag or shoes to complete an outfit. If you have a collection of brightly coloured silk cushions, for instance, display them beside each other on a navy blue sofa for outstanding **impact**, as creative livewires Andrew and Miranda Jolliffe have done in their London loft.

Brightly coloured fabric is a powerful weapon in the interior decorator's arsenal. Because it shouts out loud, drawing attention to itself, it can be used to create a sense of fun or **drama**, especially when saturated tones jostle with each other. The Jolliffes have covered a traditional armchair in pink hessian with piping in bright orange (and sometimes place electric green cushions on it). Architect Tchaik Chassay has gone one further – his sea green drawing room has chairs variously upholstered in scarlet and aquamarine velvet, and one chair covered in panels of red and blue velvet which sing out against each other on the same piece of furniture. Using fabric of the same **texture** helps unify a variety of colours. Dining chairs around a table offer an ideal situation in which colours can be juxtaposed, as in the orangery dining room of English Eccentrics designer Helen David. Each chair is covered in a different vibrant hue – gold, purple, pink, red and green like the plumage of a tropical bird of paradise. A jangle of **bright colours** is memorable – it is still perceived as the hallmark of designer and retailer Tricia Guild (of Designers Guild) some time after she has converted her style to combinations of soft, misty colours like pearly grey and pale purple.

Colour alters the **mood** of a room, and some colours are better suited to one type of room than another.

Fabrics, paint and other decorative elements in a kitchen are most likely to be yellow or in the purple/blue/green range to aid digestion, rather than hot reds and oranges, because the cooking area is already likely to be heated and steaming without the additional influence of those flame-like tints. Yellow is a wonderfully invigorating colour – it makes us feel alert and intellectually stimulated at the same time as reminding us of sensual summer sunshine – but is best used in daytime areas of the home rather than a bedroom or bathroom, where it does not reflect favourably on our skin tones. In bedrooms, fabrics and walls are usually calm, hazy hues of any colour to promote restfulness – pink, grey, mauve, green, blue or brown – rather than saturated, exciting tones. The gothic extravaganza that is Ron Sidaway's city apartment, for example, is a jumble of dazzling, regal reds and blues and ecclesiastical purple fabrics in rich, gleaming textures in the living areas, while the bedroom, including drapes around and on the bed, is predominantly restful soft mossy green.

Any room in a home can be white and neutral, enlivened with splashes of colour, bright or strong or pale, to lift it and lend accents of interest or drama. On Charles Nicholson's Thames barge the white and blue theme is pleasingly jaunty and nautical. The Chelsea home of transatlantic architects Milla and Chris Gough Willets is a lesson in using the white-plus-accents technique to make a small space seem larger. In artist Kate Blee's home, neutrals have been imposed on much of the furniture in the form of her finely woven hand-painted cloths in shades of grey, and huge grey blankets draped over sofas and chairs, with the express purpose of throwing colour (like the brilliant red pillow on her bed) into relief.

It is difficult perhaps for us to understand how colourful our daily world is in the twenty-first century compared with 150 years ago. Industrially produced dyes and pigments have transformed our environment and given us not only textiles in any colour under the sun,

but also colourful plastics, paints, paper, photographs – every manufactured material with which we surround ourselves has had a colour chosen for it, somewhere, by somebody (usually, but not always, the designer and depending on what is available). These colours may be soft and gentle, but they are just as likely to be brilliant, glowing like jewels, red, blue, green, orange... bright colours which enliven our lives. And yet we take them completely for granted.

It was not always so. Before the discovery of synthetic colourants in the middle decades of the nineteenth century, dyes were made from plant and insect material and minerals found in the ground. Across nations, the colours of people's clothes and furnishings in one area varied from those in the next because of a change in the vegetation and local mineral deposits, and the dyestuffs easily available. These fabrics faded over time. The Industrial Revolution, which began in the late eighteenth century, made dyes available to manufacturers but they were merely large-scale, regularized versions of the same dyes made by individuals in the villages for their own use. The madder plant, for example, was the most abundant and effective source of red dye, and was commonly used both industrially and locally across the world.

The story of modern colour starts in 1856, when an enterprising young English chemist called William Perkin accidentally discovered how to manufacture artificial, aniline dyes from coal tar. The first colour was a pale purple which he patented under the name 'mauveine'. Other colours, including reds and yellows, followed, and all dyes gradually improved in quality, becoming more reliable and colourfast. The hardest colour to recreate proved to be indigo blue, but this too succumbed to modern chemistry in 1880 as a result of research by Adolf von Baeyer in Germany, and artificial indigo became available in bulk in 1897. By 1913 Germany was exporting nearly thirty thousand tons of synthetic indigo in a single year.

Indigo is unlike all other dyes in that it does not need either heat or an agent (known as a mordant) to enable it to adhere to fabric fibres. A mordant is a solution containing a metal salt, in which the fabric to be coloured is steeped before being immersed in the dye. Another difference is that indigo does not dissolve in water, and sits on the fabric fibres rather than bonding with them like other dyes (hence the wonderful way in which it fades). There are various methods of extracting the dye from the hundreds of types of Indigofera plant grown across the world. One is simply to throw the leaves into the pot with the fabric. The most bizarre involves chewing the leaves with lime, spitting on the fabric and working it in with your fingers (a speciality of the Solomon Islands). Once the dyestuff has been extracted from the plant, it is soaked with fabric in warm water. At this stage it is, surprisingly, not blue but green. Only when it is removed from the water and the indigo oxidizes in the air does the fabric turn blue.

The most famous and beloved indigo-dyed fabric in the world is blue denim. There are few more potent symbols of youth, globalization and egalitarianism than a pair of blue denim jeans. Mr Levi Strauss arrived in New York from Bavaria in 1847 and moved to San Francisco in 1853. Here his dry goods store had as one of its customers a Latvian tailor called Jacob Davis. With the bolts of cloth that he bought from Strauss, Davis made hardwearing work trousers which he called 'waist overalls', the pockets of which he reinforced with metal rivets to stop them tearing. He and Strauss became partners and opened their first factory in 1873, making the 'overalls' from American indigo-dyed cotton twill, and a legend was born. *Vogue* picked up the trend in the 1930s and during the Second World War they were dubbed 'essential commodities' by the government of the United States. Finally, in 1960, the word 'jeans' began to be used instead of 'overalls'.

Denim fades over time, and we love it for that. Now we don't have to wait years for that look and feel – denim is 'stonewashed' with pumice or enzyme treatment before it even hits the shops, giving its texture added softness and suppleness as well as beating out some of the colour. The disadvantage of industrial stonewashing with pumice is the environmental cost of extracting the rocks (not a renewable resource) from the ground. In the 1970s, punk made a merit of displaying the frayed white warp threads that showed around splits and tears in the fabric. This revealed one of denim's defining characteristics, which is that only the weft threads are dyed. Denim's distinctive diagonal ridged weave is a twill, known to be among the toughest fabric structures in existence, whether made of cotton or other fibres. It makes denim suitable for upholstery and loose covers as well as all the other uses to which we put fabric in the home, and it is now available as a furnishing fabric in a wide range of colours. Using denim as a furnishing fabric (and this applies to all sorts of fabric perceived as being for clothing) is not as revolutionary an idea as it might seem, since it was current in the United States early in the twentieth century, if not before. Today, fashion designer Daniel Poole has a battered, carved wooden sofa in his sitting room which he has upholstered in a random patchwork of denim scraps. Some are dark indigo, some are stonewashed, some so faded they are nearly white. White warp threads make frayed fringes around the edges of the scraps, and red overlaid stitching outlines each piece of fabric. The effect – combining the friendly familiarity of denim with the surprise of seeing such crazy patchwork covering a sofa – is heartwarming and humorous.

As well as using denim to cover furniture, you can make curtains and cushions with it, and use it to cover screens or doors or walls. It is a rewardingly hard-working fabric that is wonderfully versatile but generally considered too rugged for bedding or table linen, though you can cover a denim tablecloth with another, lightweight, absorbent cotton or linen cloth for everyday use. Its street credentials and practicality mean that denim fits into any contemporary decorative scheme. This is especially true of traditional indigo-dyed blue denim, which has an inevitable association in our minds with the jeans that we wear. Denim is now available in a wide choice of colours, and will fit into any scheme where a matt, cotton, hardwearing fabric is serviceable, including historic interiors, but especially in a seaside or country context.

All over the world, 'country' or 'ethnic' fabric, originally made for local provincial use (as opposed to sophisticated international urban styles), uses colour and pattern as an outlet for personal creativity as well as a vehicle for making homes more beautiful. Sometimes this pattern is woven, as in the dazzling rainbow stripes of fabric made in the Andes or the bright checks originating in Îndia and known generally as 'Madras'. Another illustration of vibrant woven pattern is provided by the blankets made by the Navajo tribe of Native Americans. To look at one of these distinctive fabrics is to know at once from where it has come.

As well as being useful for the purpose for which they were created – namely, for keeping warm in bed at night – blankets either colourful or creamy can be used as throws on sofas and chairs, where their hairy surface texture prevents them slipping about. A pair of blankets can be used as instant curtains at a window or around a bed, suspended from curtain clips and a rod or rail. All the better if the ends are fringed – the top of the blanket can be folded down before being clipped, to show off the decorative fringe. Blankets also look charming folded and piled on top of a low wardrobe (with a single fat fold foremost for neatness and to show off the pattern, colour and texture) in a country bedroom. They can be used as bed covers, tablecloths (under a practical cotton cloth at mealtimes, as with denim) and in the garden when the ground is dry. When they are finally worn out in parts, old blankets can be given a boiling wash and cut up to make cushion and hotwater bottle covers. The idea of recycling

blankets, and indeed old sweaters, by boil-washing them and transforming them into something else with the aid of a sewing machine is an appealing current decorating idea related to recycling. Boiled wool fabric (though not necessarily recycled) has also found favour with fashion designers, providing yet another link between clothing and interiors trends.

Ikat is a well-known country fabric, astonishing in its complexity. To make ikat, bundles of yarn are stretched across a frame and tightly bound or clamped in various places. Then the yarn is removed from the frame and dyed; where it has been bound the dye will not penetrate, leaving stretches of yarn without colour. When the yarn is woven into cloth a design with softened edges appears as if by magic. Ikat is made in many regions including Central America, West Africa and Japan. In Japan it is called kasuri and indigo is often used to dye the yarn. This results in a once-ubiquitous family of small repeating patterns in white on blue that are familiar from Hokusai prints and old photographs of village children. Depending on the robustness of the cloth (ikat tends to be a lightweight, supple fabric with a smooth but not silky texture to its surface), ikat can be used anywhere in the home. Its pattern is quite detailed and will contribute the greatest decorative interest on cushions, bed covers, and curtains or blinds in small rooms. Seen from a distance across a larger space, however, the soft-edged pattern on ikat fabric comes into focus, which makes a distinct but different impact.

Tie-dye was a way of decorating fabric beloved of hippies and flower people in Europe and America in the 1960s. It has recently enjoyed a revival in the fashion world, but on some parts of the globe it never went away. In Nigeria, plangi decoration is created by tying cloth tightly around grains, stones or sticks before dyeing, making a cloth with variously shaped, tiny, puckered rings of white (or whatever the colour of the underlying cloth) repeated across the fabric.

Among the most fascinating techniques are those in which the pattern itself is created by the ways in which the fabric reveals or conceals itself from dye. These methods include resist and discharge as well as tie-dye. Discharge-printed patterns are created by removing the colour from dyed cloth in selected places by printing or patterning it with a bleach. William Morris created indigo discharge designs for fabric in the later nineteenth century as part of his campaign to bring the dyeing of fabrics back into touch with people and natural beauty. In his search for a satisfactory dyeing technique, he warned: 'Anyone wanting to produce dyed textiles with any artistic quality in them must entirely forgo the modern and commercial methods in favour of those which are at least as old as Pliny, who speaks of them as being old in his time.' Resist decoration is made by coating the fabric with wax or another substance which will act as a barrier when it is dipped into the dye. Batik (called different names in different parts of the world) is a resist method, as is the embroidered resist technique practised in Senegal. Here the cloth is embroidered and dyed and then the stitches are removed, leaving their ghostly imprint on the fabric like a negative photographic image.

From time immemorial, mankind has used whatever dyestuffs were available to colour and decorate fabrics in order to make them more individual, and to transform them into expressions of joy at being alive. Decorated garments have frequently had social and religious significance on both personal and communal levels. The kanga of East Africa, the design of which always incorporates a slogan, motto or even (in modern times) a health education message, is a fine example of this. Then there is the kobene, the brilliant scarlet cloth whose dazzling hue seems to signal triumph over adversity when worn by close relatives of the dead at a funeral in Ghana. Turkish suzani, flamboyantly and brightly coloured embroidered cloths which traditionally formed part of a bride's dowry and which today make fine throws, bed covers and wallhangings, are another example of fabric's significance in marking rites of passage in human life in so many cultures. The finest of all these fabric heirlooms have often been carefully preserved through the generations, so that we are fortunate in being able to enjoy and appreciate their beauty. But the decorating and dyeing of cloth is not only a fascinating part of textile history – it is both big business and a craft practised and celebrated on every continent and in every culture.

In a modern world where so much is mechanized and urgent, fabrics which are dyed or printed by hand, and those embellished by hand like the fabrics in Chapter Five, bring a personal element of craftsmanship into our homes. They bring us into touch (literally as well as metaphorically) with other ways of life and other parts of the globe. They offer the ultimate convergence of colour and texture. They are the opposite of hard-edged – they are a softening influence, fulfilling the same purpose visually as fabric does throughout the home in a physical way. The textures of fabrics – rough or smooth, fine or coarse, piled or slippery – appeal to our senses, and our imagination. Their colours and the way they play with light add to their interest for us.

The chapters of this book have aimed to show the countless types of fabric available to us in all their beauty and variety of finish, colour, pattern and, above all, wonderful textures, both physical and visual. Fabric brings comfort and charm to the rooms of our homes and enables us to make dramatic changes of mood and style, and to change with the seasons. We may want less or more of it, but it always makes a significant contribution to a decorative scheme. Decorating with texture through fabric is a joy – having discovered it, we claim it for our own and will never gladly give it up.

FABRIC
FOR REAL

This chapter looks at some of the practicalities of working with and caring for various types of fabric, and also explains some of the basic terminology of fabric construction.

WARP

These are the threads which go down the length of a piece of fabric in one continuous line, giving the cloth its underlying strength and structure.

WEFT

These threads go from side to side on the cloth, forming the selvedges at the edges.

YARN

The name given to the threads in the warp and weft, and also where appropriate the pile (see below).

FIBRE

This is the matter from which the yarn is made. Sometimes, as with linen and silk, it is also the name given to the cloth made from it, though the fibre can also be made into other types of cloth – linen velvet, for example, or silk satin. In these cases, 'velvet' and 'satin' are the names generally given to the fabric and refer to the way it is woven and constructed. These names also usually give us a good idea of the texture of the finished textile.

WEAVE

The way in which the cloth is structured by the weft thread passing over and under warp threads, often in a more complicated pattern than simply over one then under one (known as 'plain weave').

PILE

The upstanding tufts of yarn on velvet, corduroy and other 'furry' fabrics, which give the fabric a distinctive and desirable depth both physical and visual.

CLOTH

Synonymous in this book with fabric and textile.

LINEN AND COTTON

These are fabrics that are easy to work with when making curtains, blinds or covers. They should (if untreated – don't do this to cotton chintz, for example) be pre-washed, as both, especially linen, will shrink when first laundered. The traditional advice is to iron these fabrics when they are still damp, in order to get the best, smoothest flat finish. You would almost certainly want to iron a length of fabric that you are about to sew into curtains, blinds, upholstery or accessories, but sheets and loose covers don't necessarily have to be ironed. Stretched tight across the mattress, a linen sheet that has dried flat on the line or on a rack will soon look very little different from one that was laboriously ironed.

Loose covers can either be left unironed, (in which case replace them on their furniture while still slightly damp to stretch them tight as they dry) or purposely scrunched up while damp to give them added tactile quality once back on the furniture. There is nothing to match ironing, however, if you want your linen to have a glossy, burnished finish.

The alternative to pre-shrinking cotton and linen fabric is never to wash your curtains or covers, only dryclean them (manufacturer's instructions allowing). If this is your intention, and you are making up the fabric yourself, remember not to have the iron on steam setting when you press open your seams. If you do this, the dampness of the steam may cause the fabric along the seams to shrink.

Both linen and cotton wash and wear so well that dirt and spilt food or drink are quite easily dealt with. As with all fabrics, however, the sooner stains are cleaned the better. Cold water is generally better for the first rinse, as hot water can set the stain. With grease or wax, scrape away as much as possible before washing the fabric in hot, soapy water. Wax that has soaked into the fibres can usually be removed by placing blotting paper or brown wrapping paper over it and applying a hot, dry iron (before washing).

Linen is wonderfully absorbent (wet it with twice its weight in water and it still won't drip), but this means it needs more water to be washed really effectively so don't cram the washing machine full. It also gives up moisture efficiently, so that it dries fast. Using a linen towel feels quite different to cotton for this reason. However, linen's absorbency means that it is vulnerable to mildew (as indeed is cotton). Don't use it in a position where it will not be allowed to dry out, such as on a window that suffers serious condensation, or in an erratically ventilated kitchen or bathroom.

VELVET

Like other pile fabrics, velvet tends to collect dust, a problem exacerbated by the tradition of hanging it with the pile lying upwards in order to enjoy the full richness of its colour. Velvet cannot be washed, as this would disrupt the pile and remove the finish (for the same reason, check that your drycleaner uses the liquid-free method). A gentle brush with a vacuum cleaner will remove most dry dust.

When working with velvet, the classic mistake is to fail to ensure that the pile lies the same way on all the panels that you are sewing together. A panel the opposite way up will appear to be a different colour.

ANTIQUE TEXTILES

Antique textiles have a distinct appeal. Their mellow colours and the physical evidence they often carry of age and a past life contribute to a sense of history which they bring with them into your home. If you find a piece that is in particularly poor condition it may need professional repair (the Royal School of Needlework in Middlesex in England takes commissions from across the world and will give advice). However, if the piece is in fair condition, it may only be necessary to apply some common sense in caring for it.

An antique textile needs to be accorded the same consideration as a piece of antique furniture. Don't keep it in direct sunlight as this will damage it, as will damp (mop any spills immediately but don't wash with water) and extreme dryness, which will cause the fibres to become brittle. Never beat or shake violently. A gentle shake and possibly an extremely careful application of a vacuum cleaner on a low setting should remove any dirt, but don't apply friction. If possible, clean the back of the piece as well as the front: any textile hanging bare against a wall is a classic refuge for moths. Don't cut or pull any loose threads or frays – simply pass them through to the back, if their appearance distresses you. If your textile is in good condition and not valuable, you could make it into a cushion cover backed with a contrasting fabric – the ideal use for any small piece of interestingly coloured or patterned luxurious fabric such as tapestry or brocade.

DYEING FABRIC AT HOME

The range of dyes now available for experimenting at home is wide and their performance reliable. A world of colour possibilities is open to us. There are hot-water dyes for transforming larger items in the washing machine and cold-water dyes for painting on to fabric. A length of cloth can be dyed two different colours if you dip each end in one colour of cold-water dye and let it seep up towards the middle. There are fabric pens and paints for adults and children alike to play with, while the more experienced can create real batik and complex painted effects on fabric. Some general rules hold true throughout.

Always work on clean, dry fabric (unless the instructions indicate otherwise) and check that the fibre content is compatible with the dye. Don't wear smart clothes and do wear rubber gloves if your skin will be in contact with the dye. Don't forget that the colour you are adding to the fabric will combine with the existing colour to produce a result – for example, red cloth and blue dye make purple. Finally, remember to have fun putting colour on fabric.

Above: Cushions in various sizes and shapes are made with the following woven or printed fabrics supplied by JAB: (from the back) Cobra, Anaconda, Mamba and Leopard.

Below: Fired Earth fabrics – Grenadine Stripe (sea blue curtain) and Bali Organza (jasmine sheer,) from The Traveller collection and Rowan Tree (chair) from The Natural Lines collection.

FIRED EARTH LONDON SHOWROOMS

174 Chiswick High Road
CHISWICK, W4 1PR
Tel: 020 8994 5355/4353

117–119 Fulham Road
SW3 6RL
Tel: 020 7589 0489

34 Cross Street
ISLINGTON, N1 2BG
Tel: 020 7226 9700

41 Heath Street
HAMPSTEAD, NW3 6UA
Tel: 020 7345 1473

102 Portland Road
W11 4LX
Tel: 020 7221 4825

58 High Street
WIMBLEDON, SW19 5EE
Tel: 020 8879 0855

BATHROOM SHOWROOM
229 Ebury Street
SW1W 8UT
Tel: 020 7823 4549

AROUND UK

3 Saracen Street
BATH
Avon BA1 5BR
Tel: 01225 442594

23 Bruce Street
BELFAST BT2 7JD
Tel: 02890 238000

10–12 North Bar Within
BEVERLEY
East Yorkshire HU17 8AX
Tel: 01482 864878

63 Poole Road
Westbourne
BOURNEMOUTH
BH4 9BA
Tel: 01202 766441

15C Prince Albert Street
The Lanes
BRIGHTON BN1 1HF
Tel: 01273 719977

65A Whiteladies Road
(on Aberdeen Road)
Clifton
BRISTOL BS8 2LY
Tel: 0117 973 7400

3 Bridge Street
CAMBRIDGE CB2 1UA
Tel: 01223 300941

15A Burgate
CANTERBURY CT1 2HG
Tel: 01227 764944

57 Moulsham Street
CHELMSFORD
Essex CM2 0JA
Tel: 01245 494684

25 Clarence Parade
CHELTENHAM
Gloucestershire
GL50 3PA
Tel: 01242 251455

36 Lower Bridge Street
CHESTER
Cheshire CH1 1RS
Tel: 01244 348084

13A Eastgate Square
CHICHESTER
W. Sussex PO19 1JL
Tel: 01243 538523

101 High Street
COLCHESTER
Essex CO1 1TH
Tel: 01206 543525

29 Castle Street
EDINBURGH
EH2 3DN
Tel: 0131 220 2611

83 St Vincent Street
GLASGOW G2 5TF
Tel: 0141 204 0917

2 Chapel Street
GUILDFORD
Surrey GU1 3UH
Tel: 01483 300052

4–6 Cheltenham Parade
HARROGATE HG1 1DB
Tel: 01423 529991

11 King Street
HEREFORD HR4 9BW
Tel: 01432 277000

The Boulevard
Crest Road
HIGH WYCOMBE
Bucks HP11 1UA

1 High Street
HUNGERFORD
Berkshire RG17 0DN
Tel: 01488 680707

36 Market Place
KINGSTON UPON
THAMES
Surrey KT1 1JQ
Tel: 020 8549 6655

5–9 Sir Simons Arcade
(off Market Street)
LANCASTER LA1 1JL
Tel: 01524 841020

114 Regent Street
LEAMINGTON SPA
Warwickshire CV32 4NR
Tel: 01926 886125

80 Vicar Lane
LEEDS LS1 7JH
Tel: 0113 2448404

Vale Farm
Woburn Road
LIDLINGTON
Bedfordshire MK43 0NL
Tel: 01234 765765

78 Bishops Centre
Taplow, MAIDENHEAD
Berkshire SL6 0NY
Tel: 01628 661900

16 John Dalton Street
MANCHESTER M2 6HY
Tel: 0161 8323122

44 Mosley Street
NEWCASTLE UPON TYNE
NE1 1DF
Tel: 0191 221 2661

Applegarth Building
220A High Street
NORTHALLERTON
North Yorkshire DL7 8LU
Tel: 01609 774402

Warmington Mill
Eaglethorpe
Warmington,
PETERBOROUGH
Northamptonshire
PE8 6TJ
Tel: 01832 280088

7 St Giles Street
NORWICH NR2 1JL
Tel: 01603 619612

14 King Street
NOTTINGHAM
Nottinghamshire
NG1 2AY
Tel: 0115 947 6534

Hewits Farm
Court Road, Chelsfield
ORPINGTON
Kent BR6 7RQ
Tel: 01959 534 824

13 Woodstock Road
OXFORD
Oxon OX2 6HA
Tel: 01865 514549

Twyford Mill
Oxford Road
Adderbury, BANBURY
Oxfordshire OX17 3HP
Tel: 01295 914 399

21 Winchester Street
SALISBURY
Wiltshire SP1 1HB
Tel: 01722 414554

South Street
SHERBORNE DT9 3TD
Tel: 01935 817900

42 High Street
SHREWSBURY SY1 1ST
Tel: 01743 344155

38 Poplar Road
SOLIHULL
West Midlands B91 3AB
Tel: 0121 704 3605

60 Holywell Hill
ST ALBANS
Hertfordshire AL1 1BX
Tel: 01727 855407

76 Calverley Road
TUNBRIDGE WELLS
Kent TN1 2UJ
Tel: 01892 540220

2 Church Street
WILMSLOW
Cheshire SK9 1AU
Tel: 01625 548 048

OUTSIDE UK

Nikolaj Plads 11
1067 COPENHAGEN
DENMARK
Tel: 3393 9331

Koenigstrasse 5
30175 HANNOVER
GERMANY
Tel: 0511 3360508

2404 Dominion Centre
43–59 Queens Road East
WANCHAI, HONG KONG
Tel: 286 13864

31 Lower Ormonde Quay
DUBLIN, IRELAND
Tel: 01873 5362/3

Brickhouse BV
Stieltjesstraat 116
3071 JX ROTTERDAM
THE NETHERLANDS
Tel: 010 290 7050

Bygdøy Alle 56
0265 OSLO, NORWAY
Tel: 2243 6270

Chalmersgatan 21
S 41135 GOTHENBURG
SWEDEN
Tel: 3116 7520

Nybrogatan 3
S 11434 STOCKHOLM
SWEDEN
Tel: 8611 8117

This tropical day bed is constructed from manmade fibres designed to reproduce the charm of rattan or wicker and is dressed in the purest white linen, cotton and voile, but with the added qualities of being weather-resistant and colour-fast. A happy meeting of old and new, natural and manmade.

The Mengo dance company (made up of members of the Koryak, Eveni and Chukchi tribes from the Kamchatka Peninsula of Eastern Russia) perform a dance dedicated to the seagull. Meanwhile the water swirls around the rocks on which they stand, as it has done for thousands of years.

The scented mystery of exotic, far-flung locations is suggested by draping and knotting this four-poster bed with various luxurious fabrics, gauzy, patterned and glowing with colour.

Glance once and see the smooth rocks in a dry-stone wall. Look closer... and a pile of individual, hand-framed knitted cushions reveals itself. Crafted from silk and Scottish lambs' wool, the cushions are made on the Scottish Orkney Islands and inspired by the local landscape and seascape.

Texture is everywhere you look for it, from your breakfast cereal first thing in the morning to chocolates after dinner at night. Be alert to inspiration.

This wrinkled face belongs to a classic Shar Pei, a breed of dog rescued from extinction by Matgo Law and breeders in the USA. Once known as the world's rarest dog, the breed survived in southern Communist China until rediscovered by Law. Shar Pei, meaning 'sand skin', are so-called for the texture of their fur.

Smooth leather and soft woven cotton offer contrasts with the materials from which this building is constructed – wood, stone and expanses of handsome bare brick.

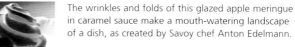

The wrinkles and folds of this glazed apple meringue in caramel sauce make a mouth-watering landscape of a dish, as created by Savoy chef Anton Edelmann.

The delicious textures of these mushrooms, including morels and oysters, give pleasure to the eye and palate. These were found in one of London's most delectable shops, Carluccio's in Neal Street, Covent Garden.

This juxtaposition of knobbly knitted cotton or woollen blanket with the sheer beauty of pure linen on a bed in the London shop Parma Lilac invites you to wrap up and lie down, relishing the touch of contrasting textures.

Is it a single fabric, a collage or a patchwork? Fabric designer Jenny Frean creates artworks from fabric fragments which are then photographed to make greetings cards.

The model wearing this fabulous sweater from the 2000 collection of cutting-edge British fashion designer Alexander McQueen is almost engulfed by its woolliness.

This exquisite image shows the fluid lines of the antelope wave inside the astonishing Chamber of Secrets, part of the Sandstone Canyon in Arizona, USA.

A single complete frond from a coconut palm has been cleverly split and woven to create a decorative fan, or simply an object of textural beauty to enjoy for its inherent visual qualities.

Another cave, this time in Norway – its smooth, pellucid, icy beauty and blue tones are a contrast to the rough heat of the desert cave above.

This eye-catching collection of cushions covered in various plant fibres and contrasting natural textures is set alongside a bolster covered in knitted leather and stacked on a hand-crafted wooden bench standing on a cowskin rug.

NATURAL

The exclusive and exotic Mnemba Island Lodge, Zanzibar, is a reef-encircled camp. In each guest hut every item of furnishing is hand-crafted, from the palm matting to the wood-and-leather weave on the day beds, which is a local speciality.

In his stunning all-white interior created for the Delano Hotel in Miami, designer Philippe Starck has made extensive use of curtains and loose covers made from the ultimate natural fabric, simple washable white cotton.

The pleated fabric on this gigantic carved statue in Sri Lanka is beautifully crafted so that you want to reach out and feel the folds. Best seen at dawn, the twelve metre (thirty-nine foot) tall Aukana Buddah was carved in the fifth century AD in the reign of King Dhatusena.

Loose covers made to fit generously can be scrunched up as they dry in order to create a deliciously rumpled texture when they are back on the furniture. Here, the rough wrinkles on the sofa contrast with the waterfall of diaphanous fabric used as a screen behind.

Luxurious textured surfaces of two high-tech contemporary fabrics are puckered in such a way that they can be pulled out almost flat. This amount of 'give' allows them to drape around shapes and curves, making them uniquely versatile.

In a contemporary re-interpretation of a traditional craft, this dynamic patchwork employs panels of luxurious natural fabrics including an alpaca-mohair mix, a wool and mohair mix and pure mohair.

This dress, sculpted from pleated polyester, is by Japanese genius Issey Miyake. The Japanese have led the world in textile art and technology. Interiors fabrics soon follow trends seen on the catwalk and finely pleated curtain fabrics and accessories like cushions and lampshades are now available to us.

This patchwork is made from scraps of checked and striped fabrics stitched apparently randomly across a plain panel of sheer fabric hung flat at the window. The curtain fits neatly between the panelled shutters so that it does not conceal their fine proportions. Other textures are used for the cushions and throw.

Patterns and textures are made by the tracks of beetles on the dry sand of the Niger desert in Africa.

Deep sofas piled with downy cushions, an ottoman covered with linen and a fur throw... these are the contrasting muted colours and natural textures used to decorate the contemporary country sitting room of portrait photographer Adam Brown.

Velvet is a perennially popular fabric which introduces a sense of sensual luxury to an interior. Some look traditional, like those with a crushed finish or in deep, muted colours; others, like these pleated and quilted velvets, are uncompromisingly modern in mood.

LUXURIOUS

A wall of padded, suede-covered panels is luxurious in the understatedly sumptuous environment created by Mark Landini for Browns restaurant in the historic Queen Victoria Building in Sydney. The comfortable chairs are also clad in suede, contrasting with the polished finish of classic damask table linen.

Rich and rare antique textiles bring history and gravitas to an interior. Pieces like these are expensive and need careful treatment to preserve them for enjoyment by future generations.

In another restaurant, the walls of a booth have been given a radical treatment of button upholstery in order to create an atmosphere of total luxury, privacy and quiet.

Detail from 'The Coronation of the Virgin', a fourteenth-century panel attributed to Jacopo di Cione and his workshop; the panel currently hangs in the National Gallery in London. Its rich surface is created by gilt laid on incised gesso, laid on wooden board.

Rich, plum-coloured velvet in a contemporary setting reminds us that deep-hued pile fabrics are not only at home in the traditional interior with roaring fire, antique furniture and gilt-framed paintings.

The Wings of a Dove, the film based on the 1902 novel of the same name by Henry James, is set in Venice. These costumes, worn by Helena Bonham Carter (right) and Alison Elliot, are inspired by the pleated silks of Mariano Fortuny, forebears of fabrics and garments by Issey Miyake.

Piling texture on texture in this way, and even looping fabrics and tassels from the ceiling as Layla Moussa has done here in her London home, creates an opulent bedroom – a bower of luxuriousness.

The depth and softness of this fur throw contrast with the smoothness of the fabrics beneath in a symphony of softness that invites one to curl up and wrap up.

The ghostly imprints of flowers and grasses are created by laying them on chemically treated photographic paper and exposing the arrangement to light, an age-old technique which combines childish simplicity with ethereal elegance.

TRANSLUCENT

Textile designer Caroline Dent has harnessed new technology to enable her to control and vary the weave of her fabrics so that they shift and shimmer enticingly. In a previous age such irregularities would have been dismissed as a 'mistake'.

Some contemporary nets and sheers are as translucent as glass and possess similar textural qualities.

To create a physical barrier that nonetheless allows some visual contact between rooms, like frosted glass but with more fluidity, hang a panel of gauze that fits exactly in a doorway as here.

Clothes are a hobby for photographer Katerina Jebb, whose style changes according to her mood. This antique French lace dress, displayed against a contemporary net curtain so that the light shows off its fineness, is one of her favourites because of its inherent beauty and quality.

This slashed sheer is called 'Swing', from the innovative range at Sahco Hasslein. Hung in a single flat panel, it accords perfectly with the cool interior created by the Douglas Stephen Partnership while, on a practical level, subtly filtering light from the white-walled courtyard garden outside.

This flawless, woven stainless steel fabric with trailing, burnished 'stitches' using a patented ultrasound process is decorated by pioneering textile designer Janet Stoyel. So fine and smooth is the finished fabric that Stoyel's customers sometimes have difficulty believing it's not silk.

A wall of windows is here unified by patterned gauze hung from a slender pole, which supports the fabric through eyelets punched at intervals across the top.

To wander through the dream-like environment that is the Comme des Garçons flagship store in Tokyo is to lose oneself in caves and tunnels created by layers of gauzy screening, curved and angled inventively. The atmosphere is serene, enticing and illusory.

Organdie or voile feminizes and makes ghostly shapes of a pair of Antelope chairs by Ernest Race of Race Furniture. This fabric treatment brings the chairs, which were designed in 1951 and used at the Festival of Britain, right up to date.

Dancer Roberto Bollé becomes something else – a wraith, a ghoul, a haunting spirit – veiled in gauze, in this Polaroid photograph by Jillian Edelstein for the Italian magazine *Max*.

REFLECTIVE

This silvery metallic fabric is so sheer that it creates softened shapes and gleaming highlights that reflect shimmering light into an interior.

This rare male *Lestes dryas* dragonfly shows off its glorious shimmering wings in County Mayo, Ireland, in the month of August.

Cut-out panels with silhouettes of flowers, leaves and stems are set between solid black horizontals and verticals to create a fabric which screens and distracts whilst letting in light while it also casts a patterned shadow onto the floor and furniture in front.

Inspired by nature and astonishingly similar to the wings of the dragonfly above, the distractingly shiny pattern on this little fabric swatch is best appreciated close up.

These rolls of metal fabric are, literally, woven from microfine copper wires on a power loom before being bombarded with sound waves – a revolutionary technique used by designer Janet Stoyel which avoids chemicals or dyes to create permanent pattern.

Take a length of wide fabric finished with glossy gold coating and simply wrap it round your sofa for the Christo effect – arty, humourous and an instant bundle of fun.

Sumptuous metallic fabrics in rich tones of gold and terracotta. From top to bottom: Rib Calvados, Chase Erwin; Bubble, Monkwell; Anaïs; Villa Nova; Brown Silk, Renwick & Clarke; Chimnay, Malabar.

EMBELLISHED

Make a shrine of your daybed by piling it with cushions made from glossy sari fabrics – the most glamourous incorporate elaborate borders and sometimes also have pattern woven across their entire length. Be aware, however, of the fragility of these lightweight textiles.

A veil of delicate beading? Silver sugar balls for decorating a cake? No, dewdrops on a spider's web, glittering like diamonds...

A sari being worn as intended, the folds of the fabric full with movement and the trailing end flying out. To achieve some of these effects, transform saris into curtains, hanging them with clips from a wire or slender pole.

Like the picture above, this is of something which is not what it seems at first glance. This, surely, is a 1960s macramé lampshade? Lamp, yes; shade... no. This lacy construction is the lamp itself, wittily knotted from fibre optics by Dutch designer Niels van Eijk.

Glamour personified. Actress Jeanette MacDonald wallows in gleaming white satin in the 1934 MGM musical *The Merry Widow*.

Monumental, red-skinned figures guarding the Grand Palace in Bangkok are faced with individually made, highly decorated tiles, giving an impression of almost unimaginable splendour and richness.

These original 1930s satin-covered chairs and pouffe by Sue & Mare are now in the Rome apartment of Valentina Buscicchio, proprietor of the shop Contemporanea which stocks the work of exciting new furniture designers.

Pearly kings and queens brightening up the East End of post-war London, their traditional splendour the consequence of painstakingly sewing pearl buttons on to garments in elaborate and imaginative patterns.

Colourful satin-covered quilts are piled up on the bed here in an equally colourful apartment where they contribute to the high-octane elegance.

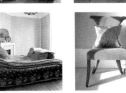

A few embellished textiles make a disproportionate contribution to the mood and interest a room projects. Here, the tone is sophisticated humour.

Crisp, calm and cool... the sheen and sheer quality of silk taffeta sings out in this almost empty bedroom by Shelton Mindel and Associates in the Halterman residence, New York.

Rich, embellished fabrics juxtaposed with apparent casualness in a contemporary interior have tactile surfaces urging you to reach out and touch. Recreate the same effect by choosing objects in a limited colour range, here gold and crimson, and set them against a unifying background.

Silk taffeta curtains in antique gold hang simply in gentle crumples in this drawing room created by Gul Coskun. They are just one of several reflective surfaces including Perspex tables, glittering crystal candelabra and the protective glass on the artworks 'Shoes with Diamond Dust' by Andy Warhol.

Soft, worn-out colours on a collection of beautifully handmade cushions embellished with a variety of stitches, techniques and shells applied to their surfaces, adding texture at the same time as pattern.

A four-poster bed makes a frame for fabric that has exceptional qualities. This one in the Saxon Hotel in Johannesburg, designed by Stephen Falcke, has pillows and covers that are hand-embellished by local craftsmen.

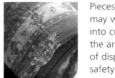

Pieces of antique fabric like this fabulously faded print may well be too fragile to use as upholstery or sew into cushions or curtains. Simply fling a length over the arm of a sofa or the back of a chair as a method of displaying it – this way it can easily be moved to safety if children or dogs invade the room.

Valuable Kuba cloths – each represents an amount of wealth to members of the tribe and are passed down the generations accordingly. The men prepare the raw materials and weave, the women then dye and embroider the cloths with earth pigments and raffia threads, creating textured surfaces.

The mouth-watering colours and the complex pattern of its interior structure are revealed when a juicy pomegranate is cut open.

The beauty of a length of Kuba cloth is shown off draped across a simple iron canopy bed frame. Each textile made by members of the Kuba tribe of south central Zaire is a unique piece of craftwork.

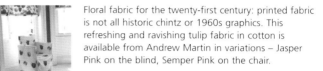

Floral fabric for the twenty-first century: printed fabric is not all historic chintz or 1960s graphics. This refreshing and ravishing tulip fabric in cotton is available from Andrew Martin in variations – Jasper Pink on the blind, Semper Pink on the chair.

Pretty tab-top voile curtains are embellished with embroidery and tiny dried flowers trapped between layers of fabric. Here they are hung to soften the lines of a severe black-framed window.

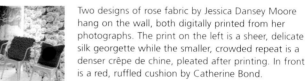

Two designs of rose fabric by Jessica Dansey Moore hang on the wall, both digitally printed from her photographs. The print on the left is a sheer, delicate silk georgette while the smaller, crowded repeat is a denser crêpe de chine, pleated after printing. In front is a red, ruffled cushion by Catherine Bond.

PRINTED

The English country home of Cath Kidston, the designer and retailer who has led the resurgence of interest in retro printed fabric designs in recent years, shows cushions made from vintage fabric fragments. One of her bags hangs from the door knob.

The colour, scent, forms and transience of fresh flowers – roses, peonies, daisies and many others – have inspired artists and fabric designers over the centuries.

Linen union is a versatile and hardworking fabric. This traditional floral design from Fired Earth, on sofa and cushions in contrasting tones, is now available in a wide range of colours. Some fabrics like this are not fire-proof on their own so have to be laid over fire-proof upholstery fabric on the furniture.

It is not only people who are bombarded with coloured pigments for the Holi festival in India. Here, an elephant in Jaipur has been specially decorated for the event and may even win a prize in one of the hotly contested competitions.

Camouflage fabrics come in a wide variety of designs and colourways, including tropical blues and even pinks and purples which bear no relation to theatres of war. Camouflage is now ammunition in the style wars raging on catwalks and in high streets across the world.

Eton College oarsmen, their boaters garlanded for the occasion, give the traditional Fourth of June salute.

Jean-Charles de Castelbajac uses camouflage on classical furniture in his home in an almost shocking juxtaposition of old and new. His collection of artwork and the Ingo Maurer chandelier (reflected in the mirror) complete the effect.

These traditionally clad girls on the island of Bali wear sarongs made from short lengths of highly decorated cotton which is also useful in the home for creating accessories like cushions or table linen or simply hanging on the wall to enjoy as a piece of authentic craftwork.

This toile on a pretty bed is in the home of pasmenterie princess Annabel Lewis, founder and proprietor of V.V. Rouleaux, which is an Aladdin's cave of ribbons and braids, fringing and tassels.

An airy, pretty, comfortable bower of light and roses, the drawing room of Horsted Place in Sussex was the epitome of *le style anglais* with its classic Colefax and Fowler chintz curtains, covers and wallpaper.

The seductive sensuality of the forms in paintings by nineteenth-century English artist Frederic Lord Leighton is compounded by his ravishing use of colour to create supple, rippling surfaces which we desire to reach out and touch.

A Moorish scene with banquettes and cushions each covered in a different fabric shows the exotic effect that you can achieve with imagination, a collection of colourful remnants and a sewing machine. Or ask a decorator to compile a similar collage of visual textures for you.

This entire room is tented with orange fabric – but not in the regimented, tightly gathered style of previous decades. Here, the fabric is loose and fluid. Cushions on the bed add accents in the same colour range and a witty little window has been cut to allow light in through one wall.

COLOUR

Splashes of vibrant crimson add drama as well as life and warmth to a modern interior that is otherwise brilliant white. The chairs, though in tune with the contemporary aesthetic, were designed in 1955–56 by Eero Saarinen, whose aim was to clear away the 'slum of legs' presented by conventional chairs.

Not just a pretty face... this heat-sensitive photograph of a human hand is a psychedelic delight, reaching out to you with its bright colours and friendly, open-fingered gesture of greeting.

Brilliantly coloured textiles made in the townships of South Africa cover cushions in the home of interior designer Henrietta Holroyd. Her English country cottage demonstrates the refreshing qualities of contemporary cottage style – a far cry from chintz and frills.

The red, yellow and blue feathers of these exotic macaws demonstrate how much more daring nature is with colour than we often are ourselves. Look to the natural world and art for ideas for colour combinations to use in your home.

Cushions piled on a chair in this manner are clearly arranged to attract our attention, rather than for sitting on. Their varied colours and designs create a patchwork of tone and pattern that is pleasingly offset by the brilliant cerise of the wall behind.

A colourful procession follows a wedding in Udaipur, India. The individual hues of the guests' garments, and their jostling, joyful juxtaposition, speak of the hopes of family and friends for the bride and groom's future life together.

Brilliant colour in the home of Agatha Ruiz of Prada. A blue sofa, orange flower pouffe and pink heart-shaped pouffe furnish the foreground, while red and white stripes and other jolly graphic patterns decorate her daughter's bedroom beyond.

Pieces of antique ethnic fabric find a new life here stitched together into vibrant cushion covers and a bolster. Even the stripy piping contributes to the patchwork of patterns and colours.

Indigo blue never loses its appeal and has links with so many cultures across the world – as many as there are regions in which the Indigofera plant grows and the dye is widely available. This cushion is made from recycled denim, that being the fabric most associated with indigo in the jeans-clad western world.

Sarongs (known in Kenya as *kikoy*), are laid out under sun and sky, searing blues on the white sands of the East African coast lapped by the Indian Ocean. They can be worn wrapped around you as intended, or employed in the home as tablecloths, cushion covers, throws or small colourful curtains.

INDEX

THANK YOU

Elizabeth Hilliard and Stafford Cliff are terrifically grateful to the following people and organizations:
Juliet Beaumont
Corrado Bertin
Felicity Bryan and her team
Georgina Cardew
Katrin Cargill
Ileana Giesen
Arnd Hobohm
Richard Humphries of Humphries
 Weaving Co. Ltd
The Irish Linen Guild
Helen Molchanoff
K Raymakers & Sons Ltd
John Scott
William Selka
Eva Shepherd at Fired Earth
E & S Smith & Son Ltd
Kristen Still
Edward Turnbull & Sons Ltd
Martin Waller at Andrew Martin

FABRIC CREDITS

JACKET – FRONT COVER

Sequined products from a selection at Accessorize – tel: 020 7331 3000

CHAPTER OPENERS

Pp 26–7: Natural and textured fabrics, from top to bottom – Rafia, GP & J Baker; Etamine, Zimmer & Rohde; Panza, Andrew Martin; Cloth Shop; Zig Zag Natural, Monkwell; Rafia. GP & J Baker; Linen, Fired Earth; Mohair, Sahco Hesslein; Linen Bee, Fired Earth; Sahco Hesslein Ulf Moritz; Ice Potassium, Thomas Dare; Silk Stripe, Malabar, Aspen Hesian, Natural Fabric Co.
Pp 50–1: Luxurious fabrics, from left to right – Falaise chenille, Nina Campbell; Fosil Oxygen, Thomas Dare; Falaise Chenille, Nina Campbell; Opera House, Celia Birtwell; Dressage, Sanderson; Fontaine-Garbo, Osborne & Little; Akilah, Osborne & Little; Silk, Malabar.
Pp 74–5: Translucent fabrics, from left to right – 8281 539, Zimmer & Rohde; UN2645/02, Romo Fabrics; Aurora, Sahco Hesslein; Euforia, Sahco Hesslein; Hightlight, JAB; Olala, Sahco Hesslein.
Pp94–5: Reflective fabrics from The Cloth Shop, except for Rib Mystique, Chase Erwin (second from top); Anais, Villa Nova (fifth from top); Symphony, Fired Earth (third from bottom); Focus, JAB (bottom of the pile).

Pp116–7: Embellished fabrics, from top to bottom – Amur, Bennett Silks; The Cloth Shop; Alina, Liberty; The Cloth Shop, Chalika, Liberty; The Cloth Shop.
Pp136–7: Fabrics with traditional printed pattern, all from the range available at Bennison.
Pp160–1: Colourful fabrics, simple and exotic, all handloomed in India and available in the Malabar range.

PICTURE CREDITS

BACK COVER

Marie Claire Maison/Eric Morin/ Christine Puech

INTRODUCTION

1-5 Dominic Blackmore; 6 Leisure Plan; 7 Red Cover/David George; 10 Dominic Blackmore; 12 Paul Ryan/International Interiors/designer G Pensoy; 13 Dominic Blackmore; 16-17 Jenny Frean; 18-23 Dominic Blackmore; 24 Joe Cornish; 25 Gettyimages/Terje Rakke

NATURAL

26-27 Dominic Blackmore; 28 Paul Harris; 29 Hume Sweet Hume/G Moberg; 30 Gettyimages/Benelux Press; 31 David Brittain; 32 Janie Jackson/© Parma Lilac; 33 Chris Moore; 34-35 Dominic Blackmore; 36-37 CC Africa/Mnemba Island Lodge, Zanzibar; 38 Alex McLean; 39 Paul Ryan/International Interiors/ designer Hang Feng; 40 *Marie Claire Maison*/Josée Postic/Christine Puech; 41 Dominic Blackmore; 42-43 Ray Main/Mainstream

LUXURIOUS

50-52 Dominic Blackmore; 53 © National Gallery, London; 54 Ronald Grant Archive; 55 Gettyimages/James Strachan; 56 Dominic Blackmore; 57 Chris Moore; 58 Paul Harris; 59 Dominic Blackmore; 60 Ross Honeysett/designer Mark Landini; 61 Christian Sarramon; 62-63 Red Cover/Ken Hayden/designer David Gill; 66 Red Cover/Andrew Twort; 67 IPC Syndication

TRANSLUCENT

74-76 Dominic Blackmore; 77 Katerina Jebb; 78 Dominic Blackmore; 79 Hugo Glendinning; 80 Network Photographers/Jillian Edelstein; 81-82 Dominic Blackmore; 83 Stafford Cliff; 84 Dominic Blackmore; 85

Christian Sarramon; 86-87 Dominic Blackmore; 88 Anneke de Leeuw; 89 Paul Ryan/International Interiors/designer Vicente Wolf

REFLECTIVE

94-95 Dominic Blackmore; 96 NHPA/Robert Thompson; 97-99 Dominic Blackmore; 100 IPC Syndication/© *House & Gardens*/ Winfried Heinze; 101 Gettyimages/Paul Harris; 102 MGM (courtesy Kobal); 103 Vega MG/Guilio Oriani; 104 *Marie Claire Maison*/Eric Morin/Christine Puech; 105 Michael Moran/architects Shelton Mindel; 106-107 Red Cover/Andreas von Einsiedel; 108 Ray Main/Mainstream

EMBELLISHED

116-117 Dominic Blackmore; 118 Paul Harris; 119 Niels van Eijk/Crafts Council; 120 Robert Harding Picture Library/Philip Craven; 121 Hulton Getty; 122-124 Dominic Blackmore; 125 Saxon Hotel in Sandhurst, Johannesburg/interior design Stephen Falcke; 128 Dominic Blackmore; 129 Gilles de Chabaneix; 130 *Marie Claire Maison*/P. Garcia /Josée Postic/ Christine Puech

PRINTED

136-137 Dominic Blackmore; 138 Linda Burgess; 139 Gettyimages/Andrea Pistolesi; 140 Katz Pictures/Donald Levenson; 141 Gilles de Chabaneix; 142-143 Dominic Blackmore; 144 Dominic Blackmore/Andrew Martin; 145 Dominic Blackmore; 146 Narratives/Jan Baldwin; 147 Fired Earth Paint; 148 Dominic Blackmore; 149 Jean-François Jaussaud; 150 The Interior Archive/Tim Beddow; 151 Derry Moore; 152-153 *Marie Claire Maison*/Josée van Riele/Christine Puech/Josée Postic

COLOUR

160-161 Malabar; 162 Gettyimages/Zap Art; 163 Frank Lane Picture Agency/Frans Lanting „ Minden Pictures; 164 Paul Harris; 165 Christian Sarramon; 166 Dominic Blackmore; 167 Kikoy; 168 Christie's Images; 169 *Marie Claire Maison*/Nicolas Tosi/Christine Puech; 170- 171 Vega Mg/Giorgio Possenti/project Roberto Cicchiné and Eusebi Arredi; 172 Red Cover/Verity Welstead/Henrietta Holroyd; 173 Dominic Blackmore; 174 *Marie Claire Maison*/Marie Pierre Morel/Daniel Rozensztroch